# Earthquake Fears,
## Predictions, and Preparations in Mid-America

# Earthquake Fears,

## Predictions, and Preparations in Mid-America

John E. Farley

Southern Illinois University Press

Carbondale and Edwardsville

Printed in the United States of America

01 00 99 98    4 3 2 1

Library of Congress Cataloging-in-Publication Data

Farley, John E.
    Earthquake fears, predictions, and preparations in Mid-America /
John E. Farley.
            p.    cm.
    Includes bibliographical references (p.  -   ) and index.
        1. Earthquake hazard analysis—Missouri—New Madrid Region.
2. Earthquake prediction.  I. Title.
QE535.2.U6F37   1998
363.34'957'097—dc21                                          97-30318
ISBN 0-8093-2177-7                                              CIP
ISBN 0-8093-2201-3 pbk.

To the men and women of the Red Cross and the Salvation Army. They are always there to help—even when we make their work harder by not being prepared.

# Contents

# Contents

# Figures

# Tables

Tables

# Preface

THIS BOOK EXAMINES recent trends in earthquake awareness, knowledge, and preparedness in the central United States, a region we now know is overdue for a damaging earthquake of magnitude 6.0 or greater. A series of events culminating in a scientifically unfounded earthquake prediction by the self-proclaimed climatologist Iben Browning in 1990 led to a dramatic rise and fall of public attention to the risk of earthquake. These events provided a unique opportunity to examine the effects of a pseudoscientific prediction on awareness and preparedness in a region facing a genuine (though not fully predictable) earthquake risk. I was fortunate to head a team of researchers who conducted four surveys in the region, the first beginning two months before the date of Browning's predicted earthquake and the last completed two and a half years thereafter. These surveys enabled us to establish a baseline of awareness and preparedness before the prediction was disconfirmed and to examine trends for a considerable time thereafter.

In this book, I report the findings of those surveys, incorporated with findings from other studies examining awareness and preparedness in the region as well as other studies of the response to the Browning prediction. I believe that this research will be useful in understanding both why unfounded scares like the Browning event occur and how earthquake information can be provided to the public in ways that encourage rational actions to protect life and property and that discourage irrational, panicky actions that carry risks of their own and contribute to misunderstanding of the true nature of earthquake risk.

Chapter 1 describes the Iben Browning earthquake prediction and explores some of the reasons why the central United States was vulnerable to such a pseudoscientific prediction. It also includes an extensive review of the literature from disaster research and from the sociology of collective behavior that addresses the question of how social characteristics and societal conditions influence people's response to such predictions. Based on this review, general hypotheses are offered regarding the effects of a variety of variables on the likelihood of believing the Browning prediction or one similar to it. The chapter also discusses the origin and development of the study itself.

The focus of chapters 2 and 3 is on the actual public response to the Browning prediction. Chapter 2 presents data on the extent to which the public actually did believe Browning, based upon both our own surveys and a number of others conducted by social researchers in the New Madrid Seismic Zone (NMSZ) during the period of the Browning scare. The chapters also examine the social characteristics of the people who believed Browning, the extent to which people planned to take actions specifically geared to his prediction, and the social characteristics associated with planning such actions. In particular, the chapter addresses the relationship between believing the Browning prediction and planning to take actions based upon it. Chapter 3 compares results from the October 1990 survey (taken before the predicted date of the earthquake) with results from the February 1991 survey (taken after the prediction had been disconfirmed). Among other things, the comparison allows us to see to what extent people reported actually taking the actions that they had indicated they would take. It also enables us to examine the factors that influenced what people actually did, which, it turned out, was not always the same as what they had planned to do.

Subsequent chapters examine longer-term patterns concerning awareness of earthquake risk, concern about earthquakes, and preparedness for earthquakes, based on all four surveys. Chapter 4 describes the trends in awareness, concern, and preparedness over the period of the four surveys, with particular attention to the longer-term effects of the Browning prediction, and the extent to which gains in awareness, concern, or preparedness were sustained over the longer term. Chapter 5 examines the relationships among awareness, concern, and preparedness, which past disaster research suggests may be far less obvious and more complex than might be expected. Chapter 6 undertakes a further exploration of the sources of earthquake awareness and earthquake concern, as well as an analysis of knowledge about earthquakes and perceptions about the local consequences of a severe earthquake. Finally, chapter 7 presents a thorough analysis of the factors influencing earthquake preparedness in the New Madrid region, including recommendations about ways in which gains in preparedness resulting from the Browning episode might be maintained and enhanced.

# Acknowledgments

I AM GRATEFUL to the National Science Foundation (NSF) and to Southwestern Bell Telephone Company for their support of this research. The 1992 and 1993 surveys were supported by NSF Grant No. BCS-9203475. The 1990 and 1991 surveys were supported by a grant from Southwestern Bell. At NSF, I worked closely with Dr. William Anderson, and I am particularly grateful to him for his support and encouragement. The conclusions in this book are those of the author and do not necessarily represent the views of the NSF or of Southwestern Bell.

The completion of the surveys and of this book would have been impossible without the help of a number of individuals at Southern Illinois University at Edwardsville (SIUE). Professors Hugh Barlow, Marv Finkelstein, and Larry Riley of the Department of Sociology, and Lewis Bender of Regional Research and Development Services (RRDS), were collaborators in the design of the 1990 and 1991 surveys. Portions of chapters 1, 2, and 3 were developed from papers coauthored with these colleagues and presented at various professional meetings and research conferences in 1991. In all four surveys, RRDS staff members provided important assistance. Rhonda Penelton, with the assistance of Pam Funk and Susan Burmeister, supervised telephone interviewers and coordinated the interviewing process, and Lynn Owens was responsible for optical scanning and a variety of technical services involved in preparing the data for analysis. Joe Stoff and Lew Bender provided important assistance in the technical design of the telephone interview schedules. Michelle Ruffner, a student whose participation in the project was funded by the NSF Research Experience for Undergraduates Program, played a leading role in the design and oversight of the 1992 and 1993 surveys. Under my direction, she wrote and executed many of the SPSS routines used in the data analysis. In addition, more than fifty student employees at SIUE served as telephone interviewers in one or more of the surveys.

# Acknowledgments

Portions of the book also draw upon findings reported in papers presented at the Research Conference on Public and Media Response to Earthquake Forecasts held at SIUE between May 16 and 18, 1995, and in the November 1993 issue of the *International Journal of Mass Emergencies and Disasters*, a special issue focusing on responses to the Iben Browning earthquake prediction. I am grateful to Samuel Pearson, then dean of the School of Social Sciences at SIUE, for providing financial support for the research conference and to Professor Ron Perry of Arizona State University, editor of the *International Journal*, for his support for the idea of such a special issue. I am also grateful to all of the researchers and practitioners from around the country who participated in the conference or submitted papers for the special issue. Thanks also go to my colleagues at SIUE and the students in the SIUE Sociology Club who worked hard and long to make the 1990 research conference a reality.

Finally, a number of people provided important support and encouragement to me during this project, as well as helpful comments and suggestions along the way. Among them are professors Hugh Barlow, Larry Riley, Marv Finkelstein, and Lew Bender of SIUE; Ralph Turner of UCLA; Dennis Mileti of the University of Colorado; and Ron Perry of Arizona State University. Comments and suggestions from Jim Simmons at Southern Illinois University Press as well as the press's anonymous reviewers resulted in significant improvements to the manuscript. The editorial production of the book was overseen by John K. Wilson of the Southern Illinois University Press, and the clarity of the writing has been enhanced by the helpful suggestions of the copyeditor, Martin Hanft. To all the people and organizations I have mentioned, and to any that I have inadvertently left out, many thanks.

# Earthquake Fears,
## Predictions, and Preparations in Mid-America

# 1

# A Brief History and Analysis of the Browning Episode

BEFORE 1989, WHEN THE American public thought of earthquake country, they generally thought of California. The image of earthquake country did not generally include the Mississippi Valley—even though the largest known earthquakes in the history of the continental United States, estimated above magnitude 8, occurred there in 1811 and 1812 (Hamilton and Johnston, 1990). There was some awareness that earthquakes could occur, but the awareness was quite limited in scope. In fact, even large-scale scientific investigation of the earthquake potential in the region is fairly recent. Detailed seismotectonic studies of the regions of the 1811 and 1812 earthquakes did not begin in earnest until the early 1970s (Spence et al., 1993).

The earliest survey on earthquake awareness in the region was conducted in the mid-1980s by Joanne Nigg (1987). That survey, conducted in nine central-U.S. cities, showed that about 42 percent of the people thought that a damaging earthquake would definitely or probably occur there by the year 2000; a slightly larger group, 46 percent, thought that a damaging quake definitely or probably would not occur. A survey of public officials involved in local policies related to earthquake hazard, also conducted at that time by Nigg (1987), showed some evidence of concern. However, the general public in the central United States prior to the late 1980s did not have a strong sense of living in an earthquake-prone region, nor was there any significant level of public concern about the risk. In fact, the risk of earthquake in the Mississippi Valley received little public attention at all until, in the mid-1980s, the U.S. Geological Survey produced a series of maps showing the levels of damage that would occur there in a repeat of the 1811–12 earthquakes, based on the Modified Mercalli Intensity Scale of ground motion.

# Brief History and Analysis of the Browning Episode

Two events in October 1989 changed things dramatically. One was the Loma Prieta earthquake in the San Francisco Bay area, which occurred on October 17. Also that month, a self-proclaimed climatologist named Iben Browning issued an earthquake prediction at a business conference. He stated that there was a 50–50 chance of an earthquake in the New Madrid Seismic Zone (NMSZ) of magnitude 6.5 to 7.5 around December 2 or 3, 1990 (Gori, 1993). The NMSZ centers on the New Madrid fault system, which extends from northeastern Arkansas through southeast Missouri and extreme western Tennessee and Kentucky to the southern tip of Illinois. In part because Midwestern geological features allow the transmission of earthquake waves over a large region, the area that could experience damaging ground motion from a major New Madrid earthquake is much larger than the immediate area of the New Madrid fault zone. This larger area, the NMSZ, includes much of eastern Arkansas and Missouri, northwestern Mississippi, western Tennessee and Kentucky, and southern Illinois and Indiana.

At the time of the Loma Prieta earthquake, vivid images of damage were broadcast repeatedly on television news reports. Images of burning and collapsed buildings, crumbled freeways, crushed cars, and frantic rescue scenes were unavoidable for several days. But in fact, the images presented an exaggerated sense of the earthquake damage (which was nonetheless considerable), by focusing on scenes of the worst possible damage. Usually, this damage occurred where there were types of construction and soil conditions that are most vulnerable to the destructive forces of earthquakes. In most of the San Francisco/Oakland area, however, conditions were nothing like those seen in broadcasts across the nation. Those broadcasts showed, in a way that had not typically been seen before, the kind of damage and injuries a strong earthquake can cause. In the NMSZ, news media ran stories on the risk of a local earthquake, and some of those stories provided instruction on how to prepare for an earthquake and what to do if one occurs.

Although the Browning prediction was made within days of the Loma Prieta earthquake, it received little press attention at first. In fact, it now appears that Browning had made comments prior to 1989 about the possibility of increased earthquake activity in December of 1990. Some of these comments were made as early as 1983 and 1985, although they apparently did not refer to the New Madrid region (Showalter, 1991b; Gori, 1993; National Earthquake Prediction Evaluation Council, 1990). The first articles about Browning's prediction for the region that appeared in the New Madrid Seismic Zone were in a Memphis newspaper on November 28, 1989, and in the November 29, 1989, *Arkansas Gazette* (Gori, 1993; Stevens, 1993). During the year between the publication of those articles and December 3, 1990, more than three hundred additional articles appeared in at least forty-five local, regional, and national publications (Showalter, 1993b).

Browning's prediction was pseudoscientific. It used reasoning based upon what sounded like a scientific theory. Browning's prediction was based on the fact that lunar gravitational pull on the earth would be unusually strong on December 2 and 3 because of the relative positions of the earth and moon. That was in fact the case. Browning's argument was that this gravitational pull would increase the probability of earthquakes in fault systems that were "overdue" for damaging earthquakes, which was widely believed to be the case with the New Madrid fault zone. However, the reality is that seismological studies had previously examined the correlation between lunar gravitational forces and earthquakes and had detected no such correlation (National Earthquake Prediction Evaluation Council, 1990).

Adding to the apparent credibility of Browning's prediction was the fact that he claimed to have predicted the Loma Prieta earthquake using similar techniques. Early press reports about Browning's prediction were quite uncritical in the way they repeated this claim—even though later, careful reviews of what Browning actually had said in San Francisco on September 16, 1989 (the date on which he claimed to have predicted the Loma Prieta quake), revealed that he mentioned neither the San Francisco Bay area nor California; instead, he talked about the risk of earthquakes over a period of several days somewhere in the world. That is a rather safe prediction, as the probability of a strong earthquake somewhere in the world in any two- or three-day period is quite high. Perhaps he was given this credibility because he made the comment in San Francisco, even though he did not mention San Francisco.

For whatever reason, Browning's prediction received widespread public and news media attention. Today, there is little doubt that the prediction both frightened millions of people unnecessarily and also made a useful contribution to awareness that the Mississippi Valley is, in fact, an area in which the danger of a damaging earthquake is very real. The Loma Prieta earthquake and, even more so, the Browning earthquake prediction brought about major and—as has now become apparent—lasting change in how residents of the

Mississippi Valley think about earthquakes. These events also brought about some, though not as much, change in people's behavior, in the form of increased preparedness for earthquakes.

## The Genesis of the Earthquake Awareness and Preparedness Survey Series

At the time of the Loma Prieta earthquake and the first publicity about the Browning prediction, I was working on an introductory sociology text (Farley, 1990). Neither collective behavior nor disaster research had been areas in which I had specialized; most of my work had been in the areas of race and ethnic relations, urban sociology, and demography. But in the course of writing an introductory text one reads about many subjects that are outside one's specialty, and an area in which I had done a lot of reading was collective behavior. It was clear from what I read that incidences of "mass hysteria" usually were less "mass" than the term implies: Nearly always, they involve a fairly small minority of the population that is exposed to reports about a supposed threat (Rosengren, Arvidson, and Sturesson, 1975). One example commonly cited in the literature is the hysteria that surrounded Orson Welles's "War of the Worlds" radio broadcast. While a number of people did believe that the broadcast was real and some panicked, the great majority did neither.

This awareness set the stage for the beginning of my professional involvement in the Browning phenomenon and in earthquake awareness in the Midwest. My involvement eventually took the form of a series of projects lasting more than four years, which included conducting four surveys, organizing a research conference, editing a special issue of the *International Journal of Mass Emergencies and Disasters* (containing revised versions of many of the papers presented at the conference), and receiving two grants, one from Southwestern Bell Telephone Company and the other from the National Science Foundation. Several of my colleagues at SIUE collaborated in the first two surveys and the research conference. I served as the sole principal investigator in the latter two surveys, although a number of professional staff and students participated in all four surveys. As no doubt happens more often than "rational science" could ever acknowledge, my involvement began serendipitously.

Having recently completed the chapter on collective behavior in my introductory sociology textbook, and having watched my acquaintances and the press devote increasing attention to the Browning prediction throughout the summer and early fall of 1990, I commented to colleagues at lunch one day that we seemed to be in the midst of an unusual episode of collective behavior. It appeared that at least a large minority of the population was caught up in the Browning prediction, and, based on what I had learned in my recent reading, I thought that it might be an unusually large portion of the population. I also commented that it seemed we had a rare opportunity to study something unusual, and it would be a shame to let such an opportunity pass by. Several of my colleagues agreed with me, and by the end of the lunch we were talking about how we could go about getting enough money to conduct a quick telephone survey about the prediction. If we could get the money, doing the survey would be fairly easy, since at the time I held a joint appointment with Regional Research and Development Services (RRDS), a research and public service unit that regularly conducted telephone surveys.

From that point, things moved quickly. Several involved in the discussion observed that the telephone companies in the area seemed to be taking the forecast quite seriously, or at the least were devoting increased effort to earthquake preparedness. This led to the suggestion that Southwestern Bell be contacted about providing funding for a pair of surveys in the St. Louis metropolitan area before and after the date of the predicted earthquake. The contact was made, and Southwestern Bell quickly consented to provide sufficient funding for the direct costs of carrying out the surveys. At their initiative, funding was provided to expand the surveys to include Cape Girardeau and Sikeston, Missouri, both of which are significantly closer to the immediate New Madrid fault system than is St. Louis. It was necessary to move quickly, because, by that time, less than three months remained before the early December date on which Iben Browning had predicted the damaging earthquake might occur.

Thus began what became a series of four surveys and a variety of other activities centered on studying the response to Browning's prediction and, more generally, earthquake awareness and preparedness in the mid-Mississippi Valley. The methods and findings of those studies are detailed in later chapters of this book. They show a fascinating picture of changing beliefs and actions, providing a rare opportunity to study the effects of a pseudoscientific earthquake prediction on public thought and behavior, the consequences of its disconfirmation, and the longer-term trend over a subsequent period of two and one half years. Before we turn to what was learned, however, it is essential to understand the circumstances of the New Madrid region that both made it susceptible to a pseudoscientific forecast like Browning's, and also in need of increased earthquake awareness and preparedness.

## Distinctive Features of the New Madrid Region

### An Ambiguous and Uncertain Situation

At the time of the earthquake scare, certain conditions may have made the Midwest particularly susceptible to the Browning forecast. Ambiguous situations, those not clearly understandable to large numbers of people, are social situations in which collective behavior is most likely to occur. Turner and Killian (1987: 53) write, "Strangers who know little about each other except that they are all confronted by uncertainty sometimes interact and become part of an emergent collectivity" that "may consist of . . . the widely dispersed members of the public." In the face of uncertainty, people often "improvise" information (or readily accept such improvisations) in order to explain what they cannot understand (Allport and Postman, 1947; Shibutani, 1966). Several features of the situation in the Midwest in 1990 clearly created ambiguity and uncertainty, making the emergence of collective behavior more likely.

### Infrequent Earthquakes and Lack of Earthquake Experience

Midwesterners are inexperienced with earthquakes, but in the years before 1990 they had increasingly heard that they were at risk. Their sense of risk was heightened by the destructive Loma Prieta earthquake that struck the San Francisco/Oakland area in 1989. A key feature of that event was that it vividly showed the destruction a major earthquake can cause. Newspapers and television newscasts in the St. Louis area pointedly stressed the fact that several area freeways were similar in construction to the freeway that had collapsed in Oakland and would not likely withstand a major earthquake.

The heightened awareness of the New Madrid earthquake risk, already being stressed by Midwestern disaster officials before the time of the Loma Prieta quake, combined with that quake's destructiveness, brought a threat to Midwesterners to which they were not accustomed. To most Midwesterners, earthquakes are something new and frightening. Although quakes do occur with some regularity in the New Madrid fault zone, most either cannot be felt at all or can be felt only in the immediate vicinity. In the St. Louis area, noticeable earthquakes occur only every few years on the average, and most of those are mild and cause little or no damage.

Research in other regions has suggested that when earthquakes are a regular and frequent part of people's experience, they do not react as strongly to earthquake predictions. In California, for example, fears of and reactions to earthquakes have generally been greater in Los Angeles than in San Francisco (even prior to the destructive Northridge earthquake of 1994), even though noticeable quakes are somewhat less frequent in Los Angeles. In Los Angeles in 1976, the pseudoscientific earthquake prediction by Henry Minturn was strikingly similar to the Browning event, though smaller in scale (Turner, Nigg, and Paz, 1986). Wilmington, North Carolina, where earthquakes are even less frequent than in the New Madrid region, also experienced a similar event in 1976, although the prediction there was based on the occult rather than pseudoscience. In San Francisco, in contrast, pseudoscientific earthquake predictions have generally been rare, and they are generally ignored or taken in stride. For example, Browning mentioned the San Andreas and Hayward faults as possible sites of a December 1990 earthquake, but nobody in those areas took his comments seriously.

The experience in California supports the interpretation that the relative inexperience of Midwesterners with earthquakes made the earthquake prediction an event that they lacked the ability to readily interpret; hence it evoked a relatively widespread response. This was especially the case because it came at a time when fears and uncertainties about earthquakes were already on the rise.

### Uncertainty and the Unskeptical News Media

The Browning prediction itself elicited considerable uncertainty, since it was based on plausible-sounding pseudoscientific arguments and was stated in a probabilistic rather than definitive manner. Moreover, in the early stages it was uncritically (and, it turns out, incorrectly) reported in the news media that Browning had accurately predicted several previous earthquakes, including the Loma Prieta quake. (This early reporting was strikingly similar to that described by Turner, Nigg, and Paz, 1986: 45–51, in the case of the pseudoscientific prediction by Henry Minturn for Los Angeles on December 20, 1976.)

The general unfamiliarity with earthquake risk in the Midwest and the new-found nature of that risk probably contributed to the lack of skepticism on the part of both the press and the public over Browning's claims regarding his track record. And when the press initially reported as fact Browning's claims to have predicted Loma Prieta and other earthquakes, it undoubtedly made him seem more believable. For example, consider the following quote from a *St. Louis Post-Dispatch* editorial on July 25, 1990: "Mr. Browning has a good record of accurate predictions—good enough to be taken with a great deal of caution. That means he should be heeded; if it takes a prophet to wake up Missourians, so be it."

Many press critics and disaster preparedness officials have argued that statements like that are irresponsible: Browning did not in fact have a "good record of accurate predictions," and, with a little investigation, the press could have found that out. Moreover, considerable attention was devoted to the Browning prediction and to more general earthquake-related issues in the news media once it became evident that there was substantial popular interest. Undoubtedly, the combination of uncritical acceptance of Browning's track record and growing attention to the Browning story contributed significantly to the widespread response that eventually developed.

An additional source of ambiguity was the fact that Browning's credentials were in fact unclear. On the one hand, he called himself a climatologist, he had a Ph.D., and he used the title "Dr.," which was often picked up by the news media. However, he had had formal training in neither seismology nor climatology—his Ph.D. was in zoology. Nonetheless, his credentials with respect to earthquake science were never clearly debunked by the press, and he was given further credibility by having served as a consultant to a number of large business organizations.

## The Lack of Scientific Unanimity: The Role of David Stewart

Further adding to the ambiguity was the fact that, while most scientists were strongly critical of Browning's theory, it was not unanimously debunked. David Stewart, at the time director of the Center for Earthquake Studies at Southeast Missouri State University and the state of Missouri's leading earthquake safety official, refused to reject Browning's prediction. In fact, he made several public statements indicating that he thought it should be taken seriously. This may have had the effect, in the public mind, of elevating the matter to that of a scientific controversy rather than something about which science offered a clear answer. One of the questions we sought to address in our second survey was the public's perceptions of the scientific community's response to the Browning prediction. As the survey showed, much of the public did in fact perceive scientists to be in greater disagreement over the prediction than was the case.

### The Initial Silence of the Scientific Community

Compounding the effect of Stewart's unwillingness to debunk the prediction was the fact that the scientific community was generally silent during the early stages of the event. According to Gori (1993: 968), scientific institutions decided during the summer of 1990 not to refute the prediction for several reasons: They did not want to give credibility to the prediction by repeating and discussing it, even critically, and generally believed that if they ignored it the issue would go away. Some apparently were also concerned about appearing to refute another scientist publicly, and some may have feared looking foolish if a damaging earthquake did occur. Scientists did not begin to hold press conferences and grant television interviews until a few months before the predicted date of the earthquake. But by then, the prediction had taken on too great a life of its own for its effects to be easily stopped or reversed (Showalter, 1993b). No official agency responded publicly to the prediction until October 18, 1990, at which time the National Earthquake Prediction Evaluation Council (NEPEC) released an official evaluation stating that there was no scientific basis for Browning's prediction (Gori, 1993; for a reprint of the NEPEC statement, see Spence et al., 1993).

### Pervasive Ambiguity

For all these reasons, the prediction itself evoked considerable uncertainty and ambiguity. It would appear that the situation was an example of what Ball-Rokeach (1973) has called "pervasive ambiguity": the inability to know how to define a situation. In other words, people "must resolve fundamental questions of meaning, such as what is happening and why" (Ball-Rokeach, 1973: 379). This is a more fundamental type of ambiguity than focused ambiguity, a situation in which people feel that they understand the problem but do not know what to do about it. According to Ball-Rokeach, pervasive ambiguity is "directly relevant to basic sociological concerns with collective adaptations to problematic social situations" (p. 378). It would appear that Midwesterners experienced pervasive ambiguity with respect to the earthquake threat in 1990: The threat was new, they did not know how serious it was, and they did not have a clear and unambiguous way to judge the validity of the Browning prediction. One easy way to deal with all this ambiguity and uncertainty was to simply believe that an earthquake was going to happen on December 3.

## Public Opinion, Social Dynamics, and the Browning Prediction

### Science and Pseudoscience

With the above-noted exception of David Stewart, earthquake scientists were almost unanimous (if at first not vocal) in rejecting the Browning prediction. In the later stages of the scare, from around the beginning of October on, they made frequent public statements to that effect. From the scientists' point of view, people could choose to believe either what the scientists held to be the empirically demonstrated knowledge about earthquakes generated by science, or pseudoscientific sources using theories that had been discredited.

To the public, however, such an either/or choice probably did not make sense, especially after so much attention had been given to the pseudoscientific prediction. One important finding of the extensive study of earthquake fears in Los Angeles in the 1970s by Turner, Nigg, and Paz (1986: 273) was that people used both scientific sources and nonscientific or pseudoscientific sources, even when their messages and means of generating those messages were contradictory. They wrote, "Our principal conclusion is that coexistence rather than polarization is the rule as far as science and nonscience and naturalistic and nonnaturalistic frames of reference are concerned." Similarly, Mileti, Fitzpatrick, and Farhar (1990: 143) found that believing in the ability of psychics to predict earthquakes was positively correlated to risk perception following a scientific prediction of a probable earthquake during an eight-year period near Parkfield, California. In a related vein, Dynes (1993) has pointed out that risk perception is socially constructed: It is a product of people's perceptions and interpretations, not a direct product of either the actual risks or scientific information about those risks.

This does not, it must be emphasized, mean that people reject science. On the contrary, they show great faith in it, at times to the point of placing unfounded faith in it. Turner, Nigg, and Paz (1986: 255), for example, found that

84 percent of their respondents thought that scientists could, or soon would be able to, predict earthquakes at least somewhat accurately. This degree of belief may falsely lead people to believe that predictions such as Browning's can be made and have a scientific basis. That certainly appears to have been the case with respect to the pseudoscientific prediction by Henry Minturn of an earthquake in Los Angeles in December 1976. The Minturn event was strikingly similar to the Browning prediction with respect to (1) the pseudoscientific explanation given by Minturn concerning why he thought there would be an earthquake (lunar gravitational pull on "weak crusts" in the earth), (2) uncritical acceptance, at first, by the press of Minturn's claims of past success in predicting earthquakes, and (3) the public's ability to remember the Minturn prediction better than other news relevant to earthquakes. Coupled with confusion between science and pseudoscience is a belief, according to Turner, Nigg, and Paz, that scientists know more than they are saying; nearly half of their Los Angeles respondents thought that scientists were withholding information about earthquakes.

This overall faith in science, combined with the desire for precise information, may make people highly susceptible to pseudoscientific predictions, such as those of Minturn or Browning. Turner, Nigg, and Paz (1986: 116–21) found that more people remembered Minturn's pseudoscientific prediction than any of the many scientific pronouncements about earthquakes that were made in the Los Angeles area in 1976. Clearly, Browning had a similar public impact in the Midwest in 1990. Turner, Nigg, and Paz conclude (p. 113) that what the people they studied wanted most was more precise information. In light of this desire for precise information, Browning's impact in the New Madrid region is not surprising. While earthquake scientists were saying that there was a 13–63 percent chance of a damaging earthquake sometime in the next ten years, Browning was saying that there was a 50-50 chance in a specific five-day period. If it was precise information that people wanted, it was Browning, not the scientists, who offered it. Of course, what Browning, Minturn, and others like them offer is a false precision.

Finally, it has been suggested that a part of the appeal of Browning and others like him is that they are seen as mavericks breaking out of the mold, being willing to take a position when others equivocate (see Turner, Nigg, and Paz, 1986: 49). Such a stance undoubtedly has popular appeal. Moreover, if the findings of Turner, Nigg, and Paz in Los Angeles about the number of people (about half of their respondents) who believe that scientists are withholding information also hold true in the Midwest, this stance would obviously be heightened.

*Significant Others and the Two-Step Flow of Communication*

Significant others play a major role in the development of collective behavior. In situations in which the mass media serve as an important source of initial information, there often is a two-step flow of communication (Lazarsfeld, Berelson, and Gaudet, 1944; Katz, 1957; Turner, Nigg, and Paz, 1986). Initially people receive their information from the mass media, but their decisions concerning how to interpret it and what to do about it occur in a context of interactions with family members, friends, and coworkers. This suggests that believing or not believing a prediction, and acting upon it or not acting upon it, are undoubtedly influenced by the messages received from and the actions of significant others.

This has in fact been found to be the case in a variety of studies. Turner, Nigg, and Paz (1986: 73) found it to be the case in responses to statements and predictions regarding earthquakes in Los Angeles in the 1970s: In deciding what to make of this information, about two-thirds of all those surveyed used informal discussion with family, friends, and coworkers as a way of interpreting the information they received from the mass media. Moreover, those who supplemented information from the mass media with such discussion were found to be more aware of the risk of an earthquake, more fearful of it, and more likely to take steps to prepare (Turner, Nigg, and Paz, 1986: 84).

Similar patterns have been observed by other researchers with respect to other disaster threats and other forms of collective behavior. One of the best predictors of whether people evacuate in the face of a hurricane warning, for example, is whether their neighbors evacuate (Baker, 1979: 21). The same study showed that those who discussed the evacuation issue with others were much more likely to evacuate. Similar effects have been reported by Mikami and Ikeda (1985). In cases of hysterical contagion, Kerckhoff, Back, and Miller (1965) have shown that such behavior spreads quickly within groups because it becomes legitimized within the groups—that is, people gain support for the behavior from one another, contributing to its spread. Similar dynamics have been observed in crowd situations (Couch, 1970). While these contexts and behavioral situations may differ from that of the New Madrid earthquake scare, the common denominator among all of them is that interpersonal networks, communications, legitimation, and modeling work in similar ways in all of them. This strongly suggests that interpersonal processes played a critical part in the spread of the New Madrid earthquake scare, and that the degree to which one's friends and family appeared to be caught up in it probably played an important role in shaping an individual's response to it.

## Concurrent Events and the Response to the Browning Prediction

Two events occurred that may have had further effects on the public's response to the Browning prediction. One was a minor earthquake, of magnitude 4.6, that occurred in the New Madrid fault zone near Cape Girardeau, Missouri, the morning of September 26, 1990. The other was Iraq's invasion of Kuwait in August 1990, which led to a general sense during the late summer and fall of 1990 that war with Iraq was imminent—and war in fact did occur early in 1991, after the disconfirmation of the Browning prediction. It is reasonable to believe that either or both of those events could have heightened the public response to the Browning prediction.

### The September Earthquake

A minor earthquake occurred in the New Madrid fault zone on the morning of September 26, 1990. This drew additional attention to the earthquake risk, but it could have been interpreted in various ways. For one thing, the quake occurred at a time of low tidal gravitational force, so that it could have been interpreted as disconfirmatory of Browning's prediction. (Browning to some extent anticipated this issue by saying that his theory applied only to major earthquakes, not minor ones, although a clear explanation of why that was the case was not offered.) The September quake could also have been seen as relieving stress on the fault. Both of those interpretations would suggest decreased risk of a major quake in December.

On the other hand, the September quake could also have been seen as a sign of activity on the fault, indicating that the "big one" could be just around the corner. Feeding this view were statements by Browning that precursor quakes could occur, although he predicted them at times of high gravitational force, not low. Past research by Turner and colleagues suggests that increased rather than reduced concern would have been the most likely response to the minor earthquake in September. During a similar period of earthquake concern in Los Angeles, a minor earthquake occurred on January 1, 1979. Among those subsequently surveyed who thought that the minor quake had any implications about the risk of another, more damaging quake soon, most thought the implication was that a bigger quake was on the way (Turner, Nigg, and Paz, 1986: 370–395; Turner and Killian, 1987: 39–40). Based on that finding, we anticipated that most respondents whose thinking was influenced by the September quake were influenced in the direction of thinking that a major quake in December was more, not less, likely.

## The International Situation

During the latter half of 1990, an important context for collective behavior was provided by the international situation. Iraq had invaded Kuwait, and it was widely recognized that war in the Gulf, which ultimately began in mid-January 1991, was a distinct possibility. There is a substantial literature linking episodes of collective behavior to times either just before or during wars. The association is commonly made to the "War of the Worlds" incident, just before World War II (Rose, 1982: 28–29; Cantril, 1965). Also during World War II was the "Great Los Angeles Air Raid," an incident in which it was incorrectly believed that the Japanese were bombing Los Angeles, in response to which hundreds of rounds of anti-aircraft shells were fired at nonexistent invaders, and sheriffs' deputies rounded up Japanese gardeners for sending signals to the imaginary bombers (Mazon, 1984: 16–19). Mazon writes (p. 30), "The dream of the 'Great Air Raid' was dramatic proof of the mass illusory potential of a people undergoing the stress of wartime." Rose (1982) notes two other instances of imaginary attack during World War II: a false belief that the Nazi occupiers of Holland were under attack, which led them into a disorganized retreat when in fact nobody was shooting at them, and an incident in Matoon, Illinois, in which an imaginary "phantom gasser" was believed to be attacking residents. A number of people were overcome by the "gas," which turned out to be nonexistent. All of these incidents have been interpreted as being related to wartime fears and upsets, and there is a rather well established linkage between war and outbreaks of domestic disorder (Beer, 1981: 56–57). Examples include outbreaks of domestic racial violence during World War I,

World War II, and the Vietnam War (for a review of this literature and an analysis of how war may precipitate domestic racial violence, see Farley, 1994).

These findings suggest that the prewar atmosphere in the fall of 1990 may have contributed to the earthquake scare, and that people who expected war may have been particularly susceptible to the scare. The latter is also suggested by another interpretation: Some people experience generalized fear. To the extent that this is the case, people who worry about war could be expected to worry also about earthquakes—and about tornadoes, floods, blizzards, and other threats (Lazarus, 1966). While it is difficult to sort out generalized worry from worry specifically related to the international atmosphere in the fall of 1990, both factors led us to expect that people who expected a war with Iraq might be more likely to believe the Browning prediction.

## Differential Response to the Browning Prediction

Thus far, we have examined ways in which several factors may have created susceptibility to the Browning prediction. These include the specific circumstances of the New Madrid region, more general features of public opinion and communication processes that can lay a groundwork for collective behavior, and concurrent events that may have made people susceptible to the prediction at the time that it was a public issue. While all these conditions may have encouraged a public response, it is clearly true that not everyone responded in the same way. Moreover, there were good reasons, based on previous disaster research and more general social scientific knowledge, to expect that groups of people would respond to the prediction differently.

### Nearness to the New Madrid Fault Zone

As noted, samples were selected for interview in both the St. Louis area (about 150 miles from the nearest end of the New Madrid fault system) and the Cape Girardeau and Sikeston areas (immediately adjacent to the fault zone). This was done in part because we felt that nearness to the fault zone might be associated with degree of perceived risk, and that accordingly, those in the higher-risk areas might respond more strongly to the prediction. Turner, Nigg, and Paz (1986, chapter 11) have proposed that in locations felt to be at high risk, greater attention will be paid to earthquake predictions and to the risk of earthquakes in general. (But for contrary findings, see Mileti, Fitzpatrick, and Farhar, 1990: 122.) Important to this issue is the concept of disaster subcultures—locally based subcultures that pay attention to and create norms for addressing the risk of a particular type of disaster, one to which the area is believed to be susceptible or one that it has previously experienced (Moore, 1964; Wenger and Weller, 1973; Mikami and Ikeda, 1985: 112).

Turner, Nigg, and Paz (1986) have proposed that earthquake subcultures may develop in areas believed to be at particular risk (such as areas with old, unreinforced brick buildings). More broadly, they propose that earthquake concerns may be incorporated into the broader culture of regions at risk, such as southern California. In the Midwest, we would expect earthquake subcultures to develop most strongly in the areas most immediately at risk, such as the immediate New Madrid fault zone. Earthquake concerns and information might be more broadly incorporated into the region's subculture to the extent that earthquakes receive sufficient public attention to become incorporated into the "public mind." An additional consideration is that earthquakes strong enough to be felt are somewhat more common in the immediate New Madrid fault zone than is the case farther away, in the St. Louis area.

In Missouri and Illinois, attention to earthquake risk is, as has been noted, a relatively recent phenomenon. It is doubtful whether this region as a whole had an "earthquake subculture" prior to the Loma Prieta earthquake or the Browning prediction, but it may well have one now. If so, we would expect it to develop earliest and most fully in the immediate New Madrid fault zone, for the reasons outlined above. To the extent that this process was under way by October 1990, it could be reflected in our survey by a stronger response to the prediction in the Cape Girardeau and Sikeston areas than in the St. Louis area.

*Demographic and Socioeconomic Influences*

**Social Class/Education.** A variety of demographic and socioeconomic factors have been linked to pseudodisaster responses. A brief review of some of this literature by Rose (1982: 31–32) reveals that social class, particularly education, has been linked to response in a number of studies of pseudodisaster situations. In general, more educated respondents seem to be more skeptical of claims that a disaster is under way or imminent. A closely related pattern of findings is that education is negatively related to threat-perception (Lazarus, 1966). For example, a survey about tornado risk taken among residents of an area that had recently experienced a tornado found that less educated respondents anticipated greater damage should another tornado occur, and they indicated that they would be more anxious than more educated respondents should they hear on the radio that another tornado was predicted (de Mann and Simpson-Housley, 1987). Such differences may occur because education teaches people to be skeptical and decide for themselves, or because it increases their tolerance for ambiguity and thus lessens the need for straightforward explanations in ambiguous situations. It may also be that class-based differences in workplace autonomy lead to differences in willingness to accept uncritically what one is told, as has been argued by Kohn (1969). Still, the relationship between social class and response to real or perceived threats of disaster is far from perfect, and it does not always apply. Nonetheless, the preponderance of evidence suggests that it is likely that those with lower levels of education would be likely to respond more strongly to the Browning prediction.

**Gender**. Another variable that has been quite consistently linked to disaster and pseudodisaster response is gender. In general, women tend to believe and respond to predictions or reports of disaster more than men. This has been shown with respect to earthquake predictions (Turner, Nigg, and Paz, 1986: 172), tornado risk (de Mann and Simpson-Housley, 1987), and evacuation decisions in the face of a variety of disaster threats (Mikami and Ikeda, 1985). On the other hand, Baker (1979) found no relationship between sex and hurricane evacuation decisions.

Rose (1982: 33) has argued that gender differences in response to threats and in pseudodisaster behavior may be linked to a socially inculcated role of passivity in women. He argues that women respond either by believing in the threat and participating in the collective behavior, or by adopting a passive role and letting someone else find out whether or not the threat is real. They are unlikely, he argues, to be active skeptics and critics of those who say that there is a threat. He posits that gender differences in pseudodisaster behavior will decline with continued movement toward gender equality.

Two other interpretations of gender differences may be offered. One is that women respond more strongly to forecasts of danger because their traditional gender role defines them as the person with primary responsibility for the home and family—so they are the ones who have to worry about protecting the home and family from risk. Certainly it is clear that, although women have moved strongly into the world of work, they continue to be held disproportionately responsible for the home and for child care (Hochschild, 1989). Another interpretation is that science is a male-dominated domain characterized by culturally male modes of thinking and reasoning, and that women distrust it for that reason. If that were the case, an outsider such as Browning who challenges the scientific establishment might have particular appeal to women because of their distrust of that establishment. Although the interpretations vary, all of them led us to expect that women would respond more strongly to the Browning prediction than men.

**Age.** The literature is quite inconsistent regarding the relationship between age and response to disaster predictions. If there is any such relationship that can be gleaned from the literature, it would be that younger people react more strongly to disaster predictions and related concerns than do older people. Turner, Nigg, and Paz (1986: 172) found age to be negatively related to discussion of earthquake topics and to fear of earthquake in their surveys in the Los Angeles area. The analysis by Baker (1979) of data from four studies on hurricane evacuation found that in some cases younger people were more likely to evacuate, but in others there was no age effect. He notes, however, that part of the reason for the relationship could be that younger people are more able to evacuate than older people. In Mikami's and Ikeda's study (1985) of evacuation behavior, age was found to be negatively related to evacuation in one situation, positively in another, and no relationship was found in two others. De Mann and Simpson-Housley (1987) did not find age related to tornado anxiety. Thus, if age was related to the response to the Browning prediction, it was probably related negatively—that is, older people probably responded less. However, the basis in the literature for expecting an age effect is less than that for a class or gender effect.

*The Attitude-Behavior Link*

Logically, we would expect that people who believed the Browning prediction would be the most likely to take actions to prepare for an earthquake or to minimize their risk on December 3. However, research has shown that there are often only weak linkages between attitudes and behavior, and Turner, Nigg, and Paz (1986: 188) have specifically shown this to be the case with respect to earthquake risk. They found that there was only a weak link between how concerned people were about earthquake risk and what they actually did to prepare. Rather, discussion of earthquakes with friends—and specifically, what the researchers called "the socially bonding aspect of discussion rather than the alarm-raising feature of discussion"—was what was most associated with preparedness actions.

Baker (1979) obtained similar findings in his review of four studies on the public response to hurricane warnings. These studies found that belief that the hurricane will strike is only weakly linked to evacuation behavior, and only in the period immediately before landfall. Better predictors of evacuation behavior are the extent of evacuation in the respondent's neighborhood and discussion of evacuation with neighbors. Based on such findings, we expected that actual earthquake preparation, and plans to change schedules around December 3, would vary quite independently of belief in the Browning prediction. Preparations and plans to make schedule changes may be more strongly influenced by what people see their friends, coworkers, and neighbors doing than by whether they believe the prediction.

*Preparation*

While preparation may have varied rather independently of belief in the earthquake prediction, there is good reason to believe that the prediction may in fact have led to an increase in earthquake preparation. Clearly, local businesses made vigorous efforts to market items useful for earthquake preparation, and there is some evidence that such efforts were successful. News reports indicated brisk sales of earthquake emergency kits, as well as of supplies such as bottled water, flashlights, and tape for windows (Franklin, 1990). One member of our research team was told that a local hardware store had sold more strapping of the type used to secure water heaters against an earthquake during the month of November than in the past several years combined.

All of these reports are consistent with findings by Turner, Nigg, and Paz (1986: 367–69) on the effects of similar events in Los Angeles in 1976. In that year, news reports circulated that a bulge in the San Andreas Fault might indicate an impending Los Angeles earthquake. At that time, earthquake preparedness rose quite sharply, although it fell again by early the following year after time had passed without the threatened earthquake and after Henry Minturn's pseudoscientifically predicted earthquake of December 20 had failed to materialize. However, over the entire study period, running from when the bulge was first reported until nearly three years later, there was a statistically significant increase in preparedness. Based on that finding and on the aforementioned news reports, we expected to find that the Browning forecast had led to an increased level of preparedness.

## Summary

A variety of circumstances in 1990 made the New Madrid Seismic Zone ripe for a widespread public response to Iben Browning's pseudoscientific earthquake prediction. This was enhanced by a press that was insufficiently skeptical about Browning's track record and that devoted growing attention to a dubious story that appeared to be catching the public's imagination. It was also enhanced by the credibility given to Browning by one earthquake scientist—even though the scientific community was otherwise virtually unanimous (though not outspoken until very late in the chain of events) in rejecting Browning. Certain parts of the public were more susceptible to believing the Browning prediction than others.

# 2

# Who Believed Browning, What Did They Plan to Do, and Why?

I N THIS CHAPTER AND THE NEXT, we examine the public response to the Browning prediction, based both on our first two surveys conducted in October 1990 and February 1991 and on a variety of surveys conducted by other researchers before and after the early December date on which Browning predicted the earthquake would occur. We shall focus in this chapter on the extent to which Browning's prediction that a damaging New Madrid earthquake was likely in early December was believed, and the social factors associated with believing or not believing the prediction. We shall also examine what actions people planned to take to protect themselves from a December earthquake.

## Methods

Two surveys were conducted, in October 1990 and February 1991, as a joint project of the Department of Sociology and Social Work and the Regional Research and Development Services (RRDS) at Southern Illinois University at Edwardsville. The initial survey was conducted to assess responses to the Browning prediction, as well as to assess what people intended to do around the predicted date of the earthquake. The second survey was conducted with the same household sample in order to compare self-reported behavior to stated intentions, to assess earthquake preparedness after disconfirmation of the forecast, to examine the effects of the disconfirmed prediction on perceptions about earthquake risk in the region, and to further explore factors that may have influenced people's tendency to believe or act upon the Browning prediction.

## The October 1990 Survey

Interviews for the first survey were conducted by telephone on the evenings of October 14 and 15, 1990. The survey was conducted by RRDS using a random digit dialing procedure in the St. Louis metropolitan area, and using a random sample from telephone listings in the Cape Girardeau and Sikeston areas. The St. Louis area was defined as St. Louis City and County and St. Charles and Jefferson counties in Missouri, and Madison and St. Clair counties in Illinois. Within those areas, telephone numbers were randomly sampled from ranges that included all telephone numbers, with known business numbers deleted. A quota procedure was used, with random selection of telephone numbers continuing until the desired number of interviews was obtained. In the St. Louis metropolitan area, a total sample of 415 households were interviewed, with a sample size for each of seven component subareas determined by that subarea's proportion of the metropolitan area's population. This procedure generates a representative sample of the metropolitan area, and ensures that unlisted numbers have the same probability of being selected as listed numbers.

In the Cape Girardeau and Sikeston areas, a different procedure was employed, because RRDS did not have a listing of all telephone number ranges for those areas or a list of known business numbers. Nor was it possible for RRDS to obtain such information in time for the survey. Consequently, in these areas, it was necessary to sample randomly from directory listings, which has the disadvantage that unlisted numbers are not included. Thus, the Cape Girardeau and Sikeston area samples are less representative than the St. Louis area sample in that they exclude households with unlisted numbers. In the Cape Girardeau area, the completed sample size was 87; in Sikeston it was 81.

In all instances, the procedure used was to ask to speak to a person over eighteen years of age if a child answered. In the St. Louis metropolitan area, of 655 eligible households reached, 415 completed the survey and 240 refused to participate, a 36.5 percent refusal rate. In the Cape Girardeau area, out of 117 eligible households reached, 87 participated and 30 refused, a refusal rate of 25.6 percent. In Sikeston, of 109 eligible households reached, 81 completed the survey and 28 refused, a 25.7 percent refusal rate. In all samples combined, the refusal rate was 298 out of 881 households contacted, or 33.8 percent.

## The February 1991 Survey

The objective in the February 1991 survey was to contact and reinterview as many as possible of the October 1990 respondents. Because our main objectives involved correlation and matching of responses between the two surveys, we were more concerned in February with getting as many as possible of the same households than with generalizing to a specific area. For that reason, as well as the reduced N that is an inevitable result of reinterviewing the same households, we report results only for combined samples of metropolitan St. Louis, Cape Girardeau, and Sikeston, for those analyses in which we compare results from October and February. It should be understood that in these combined samples, there is some overrepresentation of the Cape Girardeau and Sikeston areas, relative to the St. Louis area, because of the need in the October survey to interview enough households in Cape Girardeau and Sikeston to be able to make reliable generalizations about those areas.

The second survey was conducted during an eight-day period from February 17 through February 24, 1991. Most of the respondents were interviewed during the first two days of the period, but in order to reach and reinterview as many as possible of the October respondents, a scaled-down callback and interviewing process was continued through February 24. Ultimately, we were successful in reaching 293 of the October households, or 50.3 percent of the total. Of that number, 202 were in the St. Louis metropolitan area, 42 were in Cape Girardeau, and 49 were in Sikeston. Thus, the percentages of October respondents who were reinterviewed in February were 48.7 in the St. Louis area, 51.9 in Cape Girardeau, and 60.3 in Sikeston. The relative similarity of these percentages indicates that the October and February samples are geographically comparable, except that Sikeston is slightly overrepresented in February relative to its representation in October. The overall refusal rate in the February survey was 40.4 percent of respondents, varying from 27.9 percent in Sikeston and 33.3 percent in Cape Girardeau to 44.0 percent in the St. Louis metropolitan area.

Our objective was, whenever possible, to reinterview the same individual in February that we had interviewed in October, while at the same time maximizing the number of households reinterviewed in February. To accomplish this, we began the interview by stating that we were conducting a follow-up to our October survey, and asked whether or not we were talking to the same person that had answered the October survey. If the respondent said yes, we proceeded with the interview. If the respondent said no, we asked if it was possible to speak to the person who had answered the October survey. If known and available, that person was interviewed. If not, we conducted the interview with the person who answered the telephone, so long as that person was at least eighteen years old. This was done to maximize the number of households responding and avoid unnecessary and potentially unanswered callbacks.

Of the 293 households we reinterviewed in February, we were able—to the best of the respondents' memory—to reinterview the same individual we had interviewed in October in 203 cases. This represents 69.3 percent of all February interviews and 34.8 percent of the individuals we had interviewed in October. These percentages did not vary greatly among the St. Louis area, Cape Girardeau, and Sikeston subsamples.

One indicator of the extent to which the February sample is representative of the full October sample is comparison of demographics. Such comparison reveals that the two samples were very similar with respect to race, gender, and presence of children. There was also general similarity with respect to age, marital status, and income, with the following minor exceptions: Relative to October, the February sample had slightly fewer people over sixty-five, single people, and households with incomes below $20,000. The educational level of the February sample was also slightly higher. However, these differences were not large. Only the difference in the percentage of respondents over sixty-five, which was easily the largest at about 10 percentage points, was large enough to imply, based on 95 percent confidence intervals, that it did not result from random sampling variation. Thus it can be concluded that some response/nonresponse bias occurred in the second sample only with respect to this one demographic variable.

Another way to judge this aspect of representativeness is by comparison of response to October survey items in the full October sample with that of the subsample who responded again in February. One concern was that there would be a bias toward people more concerned about or interested in the earthquake issue, who would be more likely to respond in February. As it turns out, however, that was not a problem. February respondents, whether we consider the full sample or only the subsample of those who also responded to the October survey, were not more likely than the original October sample to have planned schedule changes, to have planned to leave the area, to have considered a December 3 earthquake likely, or to consider a major quake likely in the next ten or fifteen years. In short, there is no evidence of self-selection bias in Wave 2 with respect to interest or concern about earthquakes. Our findings in this regard are quite consistent with those of Wetzel et al. (1993), who found in their samples that, if there was any selection bias, it was in favor of people who thought an earthquake to be less likely, not more likely. Based on all this evidence, we conclude that both the overall February sample and the subsample of same individuals who had also been interviewed in October were quite representative of the full October sample, insofar as we can measure.

The number of responses on individual questions varies somewhat from the total sample sizes because of lack of response to particular items. The approximate margin of error for frequency distributions broken into percentages is plus or minus 5 percentage points in the St. Louis area in the October survey, based on a 95 percent confidence interval. Because the samples for the Cape Girardeau and Sikeston areas are smaller, their margin of error is larger: 11 percentage points for the Cape Girardeau area and 12 percentage points for the Sikeston area (again based on a 95 percent confidence interval). For analyses in which the Cape Girardeau and Sikeston samples are combined, the margin of error is 8 percentage points. In the February survey, the approximate margin of error for the combined sample is plus or minus 6 percentage points. Obviously, the margins of error are larger for items on which there was significant nonresponse.

*Surveys by Other Researchers*

In addition to our own surveys, a number of other surveys were conducted in the New Madrid Seismic Zone (NMSZ) by researchers in late 1990 and, to a lesser extent, in early 1991. Preliminary results from many of these studies were reported at a May 1991 research conference at Southern Illinois University at Edwardsville that was organized by the author and several of his colleagues. Revised versions of a number of the conference papers appeared in a special issue of the *International Journal of Mass Emergencies and Disasters* (IJMED) published in November 1993 (for an overview, see Farley, 1993). Where other surveys obtained information similar to what we obtained, the key findings of those surveys are included in our discussions. Similarities and differences in findings are noted. A listing of studies presented at the 1991 research conference and included in the special IJMED issue appears in table 2-1.

Table 2-1. Summary of Population Surveys Reported at the Research Conference on Public and Media Response to Earthquake Forecasts, Southern Illinois University at Edwardsville, May 16–18, 1991

| | |
|---|---|
| Atwood, Clark, and Veneziano, 1991<br>Clark, Atwood, and Veneziano, 1993 | Survey of college undergraduates at a university in southeast Missouri, $N = 428$. Analyzed situational and personality influences on response to Browning prediction. |
| Atwood, 1993 | RDD telephone survey, Cape Girardeau, Scott City, and Jackson, Mo., November 1–7, 1990, $N = 629$. Tested for "Third Person Effect"—that is, the perceived response of others in comparison to the respondent's own response to the forecast. |
| Baldwin, 1991, 1993 | RDD telephone survey, Cape Girardeau, Scott City, and Jackson, Mo., November 1–7, 1990, $N = 629$. Addressed "Pluralistic Ignorance" phenomenon involving perceived response of others relative to the respondent's own response. |
| Edwards, 1991, 1993 | Mail questionnaire, City of Memphis, Tenn., $N = 1,042$. Addressed December quake likelihood, salience/awareness of earthquake risk, behavioral response to forecast, quake preparedness, perceptions of science. |
| Kennedy, 1991 | Statewide RDD telephone survey in Indiana, $N = 756$. Conducted October 23–November 26. Addressed December and long-term quake likelihood, probable damage from quake, and purchase of earthquake insurance. |
| Levenbach and England, 1991 | RDD Telephone Survey in Jonesboro, Ark., $N = 491$. Conducted in October 1990. Measured earthquake preparation by a variety of predictors. |
| Major, 1991, 1993 | RDD telephone survey in Cape Girardeau, Jackson, and Scott City, Mo., November 1–7, 1990, with follow-up survey in last week of February 1991. Assessed how changed situation (from events surrounding prediction to disconfirmation of thinking) affected communication behaviors of publics, as related to mass media and significant others. |

Table 2-1 continued

| | |
|---|---|
| Showalter, 1991b, 1993a | Mail questionnaire in Marked Tree and Wynne, Ark., and New Madrid and East Prairie, Mo. Survey sent to 250 in each town. Actual $N$ returned = 303. Measured perceptions of Browning's qualifications, probability of quake within next ten years, assessment of how well informed the public was regarding the New Madrid quake risk; planned schedule changes December 3 and earthquake preparedness. |
| Sylvester, 1991 | RDD telephone survey in St. Louis metropolitan area; $N =$ 435. Survey conducted November 16–24. Measured beliefs regarding December quake likelihood, planned schedule changes, and purchase of earthquake insurance. |
| Wetzel et al., 1991, 1993 | Questionnaire administered to students at Rhodes College, Memphis State University, and Arkansas State University in modified Solomon four-group design before and after December 3. Total $N = 375$; $N$ for complete data both before and after = 280. Addressed belief in prediction, perceived quake consequences, fear, preparation, perceived response of significant others. Key theoretical concepts: cognitive dissonance, stress/anxiety. |

## Findings from the October Survey

*How Many Heard the Prediction and How Widely Was It Believed?*

The survey revealed that in all three areas studied, nearly everyone (94 percent in St. Louis and between 97 and 98 percent in Cape Girardeau and Sikeston) was aware of the prediction. In addition, the overwhelming majority knew when the earthquake was supposed to happen. In St. Louis, 94 percent of those who had heard the prediction had heard a specific date, and 94 percent of those who said that they had heard a date stated the correct date—between December 1 and December 5, or the first week of December, or "early December." In Cape Girardeau and Sikeston, 98 percent said they had heard a specific date, and 99 percent of those stated the correct date. We also asked people where they had heard about the earthquake, giving them a choice of seven sources. The majority said that they had heard about the earthquake from a number of different sources, with television, newspapers, and coworkers and friends being the most common. The average respondent in the St. Louis area had heard about the prediction from more than four of the seven possible sources, and the average respondent in a combined Cape Girardeau/Sikeston sample had heard about it from more than five sources.

Table 2-2 shows responses to questions about the likelihood of an earthquake on or around December 3. In the greater St. Louis area, about 16 percent of those responding considered an early December quake "very likely," and another 37 percent considered one "somewhat likely." In the Cape Girardeau and Sikeston areas, even more people thought that an early December quake was likely. In Sikeston, 25 percent considered such an earthquake to be "very likely," and in both areas, more than 60 percent of those interviewed said that an early December earthquake was either "very likely" or "somewhat likely." In all three areas—St. Louis, Cape Girardeau, and Sikeston—fewer than half of those responding to the survey said that an early December earthquake was either "not too likely" or "very unlikely." The combined percentage making those choices ranged from around 15 percent in Sikeston to about 40 percent in the St. Louis area. Thus, the percentage who chose the "likely" side of the scale was clearly larger than the percentage who chose the "not likely" side. These figures suggest that the majority of the population in all three areas was influenced to some extent by the Browning prediction, since the likelihood of an earthquake on any given date is generally considered by seismologists to be very low. There was an apparent effect of nearness to the New Madrid fault zone, as Cape Girardeau and Sikeston respondents saw a December earthquake as more likely than did St. Louis area respondents.

These findings are generally consistent with the findings of other surveys conducted at the time showing that a sizable minority—typically 10–25 percent of the population—more or less firmly believed the prediction. These surveys also showed that only a minority clearly rejected the prediction, although some of the surveys suggested that this minority was larger than our survey suggested. Nonetheless, the largest group of respondents in virtually all surveys was ambivalent, choosing middle-range answers that neither clearly supported nor clearly rejected the prediction. Although the wording of the surveys varied—no two used identical items to assess people's belief in the

Table 2-2. Perceived Likelihood of Earthquake Around December 3 (October 1990)

| | St. Louis Area (%) | Cape Girardeau Area (%) | Sikeston Area (%) |
| --- | --- | --- | --- |
| Very likely | 15.6 | 18.6 | 25.9 |
| Somewhat likely | 37.2 | 41.9 | 42.0 |
| Not too likely | 18.6 | 20.9 | 7.4 |
| Very unlikely | 19.1 | 10.5 | 8.6 |
| Don't know | 9.6 | 8.1 | 6.0 |
| N | 366 | 86 | 81 |

prediction—it is clear that when a "middle" choice was offered, it was the most popular one. In the two surveys that offered a clear middle choice along the lines of "as likely or not" (Wetzel et al., 1991; Kennedy, 1991), it was the modal choice, picked by 46 and 47 percent of respondents respectively. (In reality, even the meaning of this response is unclear, inasmuch as in many of his statements Browning said there was a "50–50" chance of a damaging December earthquake. Thus, even the "as likely as not" response could be interpreted as supporting Browning, though it does not indicate unequivocal belief that the predicted earthquake would occur.)

In most of the other studies that did not offer a clear middle choice, the preferred choices were the ambiguous ones, with the largest proportion of respondents avoiding a position that there either would or would not be an earthquake in early December. Overall, the studies showed respondents to be about evenly divided between the "likely" or "not likely" end of the scale. What is evident, though, is that while only a minority clearly believed the prediction, only a minority clearly rejected it, and that the largest part of the population was uncertain and was influenced by the prediction to some, though a limited, extent.

*Was the Browning Response Exceptionally Widespread?*

We looked upon the Browning incident as a case of mass hysteria, sometimes also referred to as mass fear about false dangers, and have treated it as such in previous writings (Farley et al., 1991a, 1991b; Farley 1993). By "mass hysteria" or "mass fear about false dangers," we mean a widespread and exaggerated or erroneous perception of danger by a dispersed collectivity—that is, people who are not together in a crowd but spread out over a large area (Lofland, 1985: 46–53). Ordinarily in cases of mass hysteria, the perceived danger either is not real or not as great as people believe. It is an example of the specific type of mass hysteria sometimes referred to as pseudodisaster, a situation in which the public incorrectly believes that a disaster is either under way or imminent (Rose, 1982: 25–26). In such situations, people not only believe they are in danger when they are not but also take actions on the basis of this perceived danger. These may include flight reactions as well as visible manifestations of concern, fear, and, in the most extreme cases, terror.

The findings described above suggest that, relative to other incidents of mass hysteria in the past, the proportion of the population that was influenced by the Browning prediction was quite large. It is a reasonable inference from the surveys that around half of the population gave some credibility to the prediction, and, as noted above, 10–25 percent believed it quite unambiguously. Only a minority clearly rejected it. Virtually everyone was aware of it. It appears that this constitutes a somewhat more widespread response than in most past cases of mass hysteria. It can be contrasted, for example, with the highly publicized response to Orson Welles's "War of the Worlds" broadcast in 1938. Although some estimates have placed the number who believed the events described in the broadcast as high as 25 percent of those who heard it, analyses of public opinion surveys suggest that the actual percentage was far smaller, possibly as low as 2 percent (Cantril, 1965; Rosengren et al., 1975). Moreover, compared to the Browning prediction, a far smaller percentage of the population heard the Welles radio drama. As noted above, nearly everyone in the New Madrid region had heard about the Browning prediction, owing to news media coverage that was both ubiquitous and ongoing. Reviews of studies of mass hysteria and pseudodisaster by Rose (1982: 30–31) and Lofland (1985: 49–53) suggest that the maximum proportion of the population participating in any of the incidents reviewed was around 25 percent, and in most cases was well below that figure. Rose does caution, however, that after-the-fact surveys may understate participation somewhat, since people may not want to admit having been caught up in a false alarm.

Other pseudoscientific or nonscientific earthquake predictions have occurred as well, creating pseudodisaster situations similar to the Browning situation. We have already noted Henry Minturn's 1976 pseudoscientific prediction in Los Angeles; in the same year a psychic, Clarissa Bernhardt, predicted an earthquake in Wilmington, North Carolina. There were also pseudoscientific earthquake predictions for West Coast earthquakes in 1982 and again in 1991, and for a damaging earthquake in Portland, Oregon, in 1993 (Showalter, 1994; see also Gori, 1993). Did these events provoke responses as widespread as those of the Browning incident?

The most thoroughly studied of these events was the Minturn prediction for Los Angeles, which was one of several public announcements regarding earthquakes that were studied by Turner, Nigg, and Paz (1986). They found that about 87 percent of the population had heard one of the announcements (most often, the Minturn prediction), and that about 32 percent had taken one or more of these announcements either "quite seriously" (13.4 percent) or "somewhat seriously" (18.4 percent). Both the percentage who heard the predictions and the percentage who took them seriously are moderately lower than we found in the case of the Browning prediction, again suggesting that the Browning prediction precipitated a somewhat more widespread response.

A note of caution is needed when making this comparison, however. Turner's data were collected after the Minturn prediction had been disconfirmed. In our February survey, we found that about 35 percent of respondents said they had been "very concerned" or "somewhat concerned" about a December earthquake. Although being concerned and taking a prediction seriously are not identical, our after-the-fact figures are quite close to Turner's, suggesting that the response to the Minturn prediction and related events may have been almost as great as the response to the Browning prediction. Again, as suggested by Rose, involvement may be understated in after-the-fact surveys. Our findings support this notion, since the proportion reporting concern about the Browning prediction after the fact is significantly lower than the proportion who, at the time the prediction was made, viewed a December quake as at least somewhat likely. Thus, it could be that the Minturn prediction and other earthquake-related news items in Los Angeles in 1976 provoked about as much concern as did the Browning prediction.

A key factor in the public attention to both the Minturn and Browning predictions appears to be that in the early stages of news media attention to them, the media uncritically (and, as it turns out, inaccurately) reported that both Browning and Minturn had correctly predicted previous earthquakes (Turner, Nigg, and Paz, 1986: 48–49; Showalter, 1994; Shipman, Fowler, and Shain,

1993; Dearing and Kamierczak, 1993; Farley, 1993). These reports were later corrected by the media, but by then the word was out that someone with a proven track record, in the words of Turner, Nigg, and Paz (1986: 46), "had predicted this quake on the news and that it had occurred as predicted." The reports were accompanied by the message that "his prediction for December involves us." News media reporting on previous successful predictions may have created an unusual degree of credibility in the public mind and provoked a larger response than is typical in pseudodisasters.

Whether or not the Browning prediction was more widely believed in than the Minturn prediction, it is clear that the time period during which public opinion was widely influenced by Browning's prediction was longer than that for Minturn. The Browning prediction had become a major news item by early September, and it remained the focus of heavy public and media attention for three months. Our survey was conducted in mid-October, more than six weeks before the predicted earthquake. The entire Minturn episode, in contrast, lasted less than six weeks. The first news media reports concerning Minturn's prediction for Los Angeles appeared on November 11, 1976; his predicted earthquake date was December 20. The Browning prediction was the object of heavy media attention for more than twice that length of time, from early September until the predicted earthquake date of December 2 or 3, 1990. The first press reports concerning Browning's prediction appeared more than a year before the date he had predicted for the earthquake, in November 1989 (Spence et al., 1993: 4).

Although the Minturn event itself was of shorter duration than the Browning event, it was part of a series of earthquake-related statements, predictions, and near-predictions that drew media attention in southern California during the mid-1970s. Thus, the Minturn prediction, like the Browning prediction, occurred during an extended period of heightened media attention to earthquake risk, and that may account for the fairly widespread response to both predictions.

Survey evidence on other pseudoscientific and nonscientific earthquake predictions ranges from limited to nonexistent, but there was clearly less media coverage of those events than of the Browning episode, and less public attention generally.

Although it appears that there was more public response to the Browning prediction than to most past instances of mass hysteria, including past earthquake predictions (both pseudoscientific and nonscientific), the extent to which that may be the case cannot be precisely assessed because of differences in measuring techniques. The relatively extensive response to the Browning prediction, however, may be attributed to the factors outlined in chapter 1, including inexperience with earthquakes in the central United States, the effects of the Loma Prieta earthquake, extensive and unskeptical news media coverage, and the effects of the minor New Madrid earthquake on September 26, 1990.

## Did People Plan Schedule Changes Around December 3?

Another indication of the widespread response to the prediction can be seen in the number of people who said that they were planning to make changes in their normal schedules around December 3, shown in table 2-3. About one-fourth of those surveyed in the St. Louis area and half of those surveyed in the Cape Girardeau and Sikeston areas indicated such plans. A much smaller number went so far as to indicate that they planned to leave the area (see table 2-4). In the St. Louis area, about one household out of every twenty indicated plans to leave. However, in Cape Girardeau and Sikeston, the percentage was higher. About 13 percent of households in Cape Girardeau and more than 20 percent in Sikeston indicated that they planned to leave the area around December 3. These findings again suggest that the response to the Browning prediction was unusually widespread, with up to half of respondents in some areas planning schedule changes, and up to 20 percent planning to leave the area. Usually such episodes involve smaller proportions of the population.

Table 2-5 reveals that only a minority of respondents reported that most of their friends and neighbors were planning to change their normal schedules

Table 2-3. Percentage Indicating That Respondent or Members of Family Planned Changes in Schedule Around December 3 (October 1990)

|  | St. Louis Area (%) | Cape Girardeau Area (%) | Sikeston Area (%) |
|---|---|---|---|
| Yes | 25.5 | 44.8 | 51.9 |
| No | 72.0 | 52.9 | 45.7 |
| Don't know | 2.5 | 2.3 | 2.5 |
| N | 404 | 87 | 81 |

Table 2-4. Percentage Indicating That Respondent or Members of Family Planned to Leave the Area Around December 3 (October 1990)

|  | St. Louis Area (%) | Cape Girardeau Area (%) | Sikeston Area (%) |
|---|---|---|---|
| Yes | 4.8 | 13.1 | 20.5 |
| No | 95.2 | 86.9 | 79.5 |
| N | 397 | 84 | 79 |

Table 2-5. Percentage Responding Positively to Selected Items

|  | St. Louis Area (%) | Cape Girardeau Area (%) | Sikeston Area (%) |
|---|---|---|---|
| Most friends and neighbors are changing schedule around December 3 | 12.0 | 35.7 | 46.9 |
| Employers are changing schedule around December 3 | 15.7 | 25.0 | 41.0 |
| Schools are changing schedule around December 3 | 25.4 | 90.8 | 86.3 |
| They felt September earthquake | 15.9 | 79.5 | 67.1 |
| September earthquake changed their thinking about the likelihood of a December earthquake | 32.5 | 58.6 | 57.3 |
| People are overreacting to the December earthquake forecast | 42.8 | 58.1 | 46.9 |

around December 3, or that their employers planned changes in work schedules. There were, however, differences by location: Respondents in the Sikeston area were most likely to report such planned changes (friends/ neighbors 47 percent, employers 41 percent), and respondents in the St. Louis area were least likely to do so (friends/neighbors 12 percent, employers 16 percent). Only 25 percent of respondents in the St. Louis area reported that schools in their community were going to close, but 91 percent of Cape Girardeau respondents and 86 percent of Sikeston respondents said that their schools were closing. In fact, Cape Girardeau public schools and many other school districts in southeast Missouri did close; the overwhelming majority of schools in the St. Louis metropolitan area did not.

Finally, the survey results make it clear that many respondents felt that people were overreacting to the earthquake prediction (see table 2-5). Significantly, people were most likely to feel this way in the Cape Girardeau and Sikeston areas, where reaction to the prediction was generally stronger than it was in the St. Louis area. A related finding of other studies conducted at the time of the prediction is that, as widespread as public reaction was, most people believed that it was even more widespread (Baldwin, 1993; Atwood, 1993). Consistently, the percentage of people in those surveys who said that other people believed the Browning prediction was greater than the percentage who said that they believed it themselves. As I have suggested elsewhere (Farley, 1993), this phenomenon might account to some degree for the high level of mass media attention given to the Browning event. In effect, the media were telling their audience exactly what most people expected to hear and believed to be true: that the Browning prediction was eliciting considerable fear and concern among the public. By so doing, the media may have appealed to its audience by confirming most people's beliefs about how others were reacting to the prediction. While that was true, it is also true that the response was not as widespread as most people believed.

*Correlates of Believing the Prediction*

Table 2-6 presents cross-tabulations of a number of personal and environmental characteristics with respondents' perceptions of the likelihood of an earthquake. The data are reported separately for the St. Louis area and a combined Cape Girardeau/Sikeston sample. Although a sizable percentage of all population groups apparently believed the Browning prediction, the survey indicates that the prediction was taken more seriously by women than by men, and that it was less widely believed by college graduates than those without a college education. These findings are generally consistent with the past findings of other researchers. Research has shown that, both in the case of mass hysteria or pseudodisaster and in situations of genuine threat, women, younger people, and people with lower levels of education react most strongly. We shall now examine the findings in table 2-6 more closely and place them in the context of past research.

**Education.** Our survey shows quite clearly that response to the Browning prediction was strongly influenced by level of education. In particular, college graduates were much less likely than others to believe the prediction. This can be seen in the combined percentage of people considering a December earthquake either as "very likely" or "somewhat likely," as shown by education level in table 2-6. Although the relationship between education and belief in the prediction is weak among those with less than a college education in both the St. Louis area and Cape Girardeau/Sikeston, the difference between college graduates and all others is large and consistent. Apparently, college graduates had a skepticism about Browning much greater than that found among people with lesser levels of education.

Past research has been fairly consistent in showing that those with less education respond more strongly in situations of perceived threat than those with higher levels of education, although most other studies have not found the effects to be so specifically centered on college graduation. Rose (1982: 31), for example, reviews a variety of outbreaks of mass hysteria in which people of lower educational levels were shown to have been more likely to become involved. More generally, low levels of education have been associated with higher levels of threat-perception (Lazarus, 1966), even in situations where the risk is real albeit uncertain. For example, a study of an area that had experienced a tornado found greater anticipation of damage from a potential future tornado and greater anxiety in response to a possible tornado prediction among people with lower levels of education (de Mann and Simpson-Housley, 1987).

In a sense, these findings are not surprising. Education has generally been shown to make people more skeptical and more inclined to question the

Table 2-6. Percentage of Various Population Groups That Thought a Quake Was "Very Likely" or "Somewhat Likely" Around December 3

| | St. Louis Area (%) | Cape Girardeau/ Sikeston Areas (%) |
|---|---|---|
| Men | 48.7 | 52.2 |
| Women | 64.1 | 82.7 |
| | $N = 330$  Chi$^2$ = 6.82 <br> df = 1   p < .009 | $N = 144$  Chi$^2$ = 13.22 <br> df = 1   p < .0003 |
| Ages 18–29 | 70.6 | 77.8 |
| Ages 30–49 | 58.2 | 66.2 |
| Ages 50–64 | 50.9 | 65.0 |
| Ages 65 and over | 46.2 | 90.0 |
| | N = 322   Chi$^2$ = 8.94 <br> df = 3   p < .04 | N = 140   Chi$^2$ = 3.87 <br> df = 3   n.s. |
| College graduate | 43.2 | 54.0 |
| Some college | 68.8 | 78.8 |
| High school graduate | 57.6 | 77.4 |
| Some high school or less | 77.3 | 76.9 |
| | N = 320   Chi$^2$ = 17.19 <br> df = 3   p < .0006 | N = 133   Chi$^2$ = 7.61 <br> df = 3   p < .06 |
| Most friends changing schedule | 81.4 | 82.0 |
| Some friends changing schedule | 61.3 | 68.7 |
| No friends changing schedule | 47.2 | 60.0 |
| | N = 321   Chi$^2$ = 16.31 <br> df = 2   p < .0003 | N = 143   Chi$^2$ = 4.45 <br> df = 2   p < .11 |

Table 2-6 continued

| | | |
|---|---|---|
| Employers changing schedule | 77.1 | 81.3 |
| Employers not changing schedule | 55.7 | 66.7 |
| | $N = 304$  Chi$^2$ = 7.18<br>df = 1  p < .008 | $N = 138$  Chi$^2$ = 2.60<br>df = 1  p < .11 |
| Felt September quake | 66.0 | 73.4 |
| Did not feel September quake | 56.3 | 67.6 |
| | $N = 323$  Chi$^2$ = 1.35<br>df = 1  n.s. | $N = 143$  Chi$^2$ = 0.19<br>df = 1  n.s. |
| Quake changed thinking | 74.0 | 80.9 |
| Quake did not change thinking | 50.3 | 58.7 |
| | $N = 317$  Chi$^2$ = 15.30<br>df = 1  p < .0001 | $N = 142$  Chi$^2$ = 7.39<br>df = 1  p < .007 |
| War with Iraq likely | 63.9 | 81.1 |
| War with Iraq not likely | 49.0 | 62.0 |
| | $N = 276$  Chi$^2$ = 5.33<br>df = 1  p < .03 | $N = 119$  Chi$^2$ = 4.48<br>df = 1  p < .04 |
| Scientists good information source | 60.9 | 74.0 |
| Scientists fair information source | 50.0 | 74.6 |
| Scientists poor information source | 33.3 | 33.3 |
| | $N = 326$  Chi$^2$ = 4.05<br>df = 2  n.s. | $N = 143$  Chi$^2$ = 2.57<br>df = 2  n.s. |

Table 2-6 continued

| | | |
|---|---|---|
| Government good information source | 69.2 | 71.4 |
| Government fair information source | 56.7 | 72.7 |
| Government poor information source | 51.3 | 73.1 |

| | | |
|---|---|---|
| | $N = 316$   Chi$^2$ = 5.53<br>df = 2    p < .07 | $N = 142$   Chi$^2$ = 0.03<br>df = 2    n.s. |

| | | |
|---|---|---|
| Business good information source | 72.1 | 94.7 |
| Business fair information source | 70.5 | 73.3 |
| Business poor information source | 44.7 | 63.9 |

| | | |
|---|---|---|
| | $N = 318$   Chi$^2$ = 22.73<br>df = 2    p < .0001 | $N = 140$   Chi$^2$ = 6.91<br>df = 2    p < .04 |

| | | |
|---|---|---|
| TV chief information source | 54.6 | 75.9 |
| Newspapers chief information source | 58.7 | 73.0 |
| Radio chief information source | 48.6 | 25.0 |
| Family, co-workers, friends chief information source | 73.7 | 73.9 |
| Schools or employers chief information source | 75.0 | 50.0 |

| | | |
|---|---|---|
| | $N = 322$   Chi$^2$ = 7.70<br>df = 4    p < .11 | $N = 145$   Chi$^2$ = 5.58<br>df = 4    n.s. |

reasoning or evidence behind information they are given. Tolerance for ambiguity, as well as the use of thinking and reasoning processes similar to those used by scientists, increase with educational level. For example, studies by Herbert Hyman and his colleagues have found that people with higher levels of education place a greater value on understanding "how and why things happen" and are more likely to seek out information on their own regarding public issues (Hyman and Wright, 1979; Hyman, Wright, and Reed, 1975). Thus, the less educated may be more inclined to take any kind of warning at face value, and may also be more inclined to take a warning—legitimate or not—as meaning that the disaster about which they have been warned is going to happen. In contrast, those with more education will respond with more skepticism and will treat even warnings seen as legitimate as only probabilistic rather than as signs of certain disaster.

A Browning or Minturn may appeal to the less educated precisely because of the clear, unambiguous message they offer—expect an earthquake on a certain date. In contrast, statements by scientists are usually made in terms of probabilities over an extended period—in other words, they offer no clear or unambiguous statement of what is going to happen, and their meaning often seems fuzzy or unclear. Given the desire for a clear, unambiguous statement that is likely to be stronger among the less educated, a pseudoscientific prediction like that of Browning or Minturn may be exactly the kind that provides the clarity and lack of ambiguity that many people are looking for.

That such an unambiguous prediction is not scientifically well founded may matter little: The scientific method is not well understood by people in general, and it is particularly unfamiliar to those with lower-than-average levels of education. What matters much more is that a Browning or Minturn offers a clear answer, and that answer is based on an argument that the forecaster describes as being "scientific" and presents in terms that sound scientific. The notion that lunar gravitational forces could trigger an earthquake sounds both scientific and plausible, and to those who are knowledgeable in neither seismology nor the scientific method, the fact that the theory has been tested and found wanting is little known and little understood. Undoubtedly, offering a simple answer and sounding scientific make people like Browning and Minturn appealing to many. The fact that people without much education generally believe in science even though they do not understand it undoubtedly makes them even more vulnerable to people like Browning and Minturn.

In the case of Browning, it appears that education offered a significant inoculation against this susceptibility only at the level of college graduate. Perhaps only at that level does education encourage independent thinking and reasoning, as opposed to merely feeding back the "right answer" (on this point, see Bowles and Gintis, 1976).

**Gender**. Gender is also clearly correlated to how people responded to the Browning prediction. The proportion of women viewing a December quake as at least somewhat likely exceeded the proportion of men with such an opinion by more than 25 percentage points in St. Louis and more than 30 points in Cape Girardeau and Sikeston. Similar findings were obtained in a survey of southeast Missouri college students by Clark, Atwood, and Veneziano (1993). Again, as noted in chapter 1, this is consistent with past research. Gender, like education, has been linked quite persistently to involvement in pseudo-disaster situations and to levels of threat-perception. Rose's review (1982) showed that in virtually all pseudo-disaster situations, women were more likely than men to believe that a dangerous condition was occurring or imminent, whereas men were more likely to take the role of skeptic. Rose states (p. 32) that this reflects effects of "the traditional female role of relative passivity and suggestibility as opposed to the aggressiveness and autonomy of the traditional male role." As was noted in chapter 1, he also suggests that "greater female participation in mass hysteria may well disappear as women's liberation progresses." Our own findings suggest, however, that the effects of traditional gender roles still influenced pseudo-disaster behavior in the central United States in 1990.
We suggested in chapter 1, however, that other aspects of gender roles may also have acted to produce the differences we measured. For one, traditional gender roles give women the primary responsibility for the home and family—thus, they would be the ones to worry about protecting the home and family from risk. Certainly research has demonstrated that even as women have moved en masse into the paid labor force, they continue to be held disproportionately responsible for the home and for child care (Hochschild, 1989; Zhang and Farley, 1995).
The findings of Turner, Nigg, and Paz (1986) in Los Angeles support these interpretations. They found that gender had an indirect effect on whether or

not people took earthquake predictions seriously (which of several predictions was not specified, but most often people recalled Minturn's). This indirect effect occurred because women were more fearful than men about earthquakes, and to a lesser extent because women were more likely than men to discuss earthquake-related topics. The former indirect effect is consistent with Rose's interpretation as outlined above, whereas the latter may reflect a tendency to discuss and address a risk to home and family.

**Trust in Science.** As was suggested in chapter 1, an alternative interpretation of our findings regarding gender is that science is a male-dominated domain characterized by culturally male modes of thinking and reasoning, and that women distrust it for that reason. In the case of the 1976 Minturn earthquake prediction in Los Angeles, it is clear that part of Minturn's appeal was that he was a maverick, offering an alternative to the often fuzzy, cautious, and qualified statements made by science (Turner, Nigg, and Paz, 1986). We believe that this was also much of the basis of Browning's appeal. While this was undoubtedly part of his appeal in general, it may have been particularly appealing to women. If it is true that women particularly distrust the scientific establishment, then a maverick like Minturn or Browning may be more appealing to them than to men, who may identify more with science and technology and thus trust scientists to a greater extent.

In a similar vein, distrust of scientists may also explain some of the reason why those with less than a college education found Browning more appealing. Turner, Nigg, and Paz (1986: 49) aptly describe this phenomenon in explaining the response to Henry Minturn's pseudoscientific prediction of an earthquake in Los Angeles in 1976:

> Minturn was an apt symbol for the well-known populist theme in American culture. He was a maverick, not associated with "big science." He showed the world that truth was much simpler than the experts made it seem. He demonstrated that a resourceful person relying substantially on common sense could solve problems that remained insoluble to professionals whose methods and laboratories kept them out of touch with the real world. To the most confirmed populists, he was even more impressive when stripped of his

educational credentials, for he now became the truly self-made man. And he asked only to be judged by his success in predicting earthquakes, not by theories and professional collegiality. Once this image was set, one could hardly be surprised that the experts, still unsuccessful in their own efforts to predict earthquakes, should attempt to discredit Minturn.

Although Turner, Nigg, and Paz were writing in 1976 about Minturn, every word of the passage above could be applied to Browning in 1990. Clearly, the fact that Browning could offer simple answers about earthquakes, with specific dates and places—which earthquake scientists could not do—made Browning appealing. One could argue that this would be particularly the case for people already predisposed to distrust science. And if the kind of populist distrust of science that Turner, Nigg, and Paz describe is more common among women and among people without college degrees, this might well explain why these groups were more likely to believe Browning.

**Perceptions about the Reaction of Science to Browning's Prediction.** Our data suggest, however, that to view the Browning event only in the way described above is to miss an important part of the dynamic. For one thing, many people did not see Browning as a critic of science or as an alternative to science: Many people viewed him as a scientist, and apparently many viewed the disagreement between Browning and his scientific critics as a legitimate scientific dispute. We asked our respondents in the February 1991 survey what they thought the December earthquake predictor's occupation was. A plurality of respondents, both in the St. Louis area (33 percent) and in Cape Girardeau and Sikeston (43 percent), answered "scientist." Although less than half gave this answer, it was given more often than any other answer. Thus, it is clear that a number of people did think of Browning as a scientist. (The next most common answer was "weatherman," at 25 percent in the St. Louis area and 14 percent in Cape Girardeau and Sikeston.)

In addition, it is clear that people were very confused about the response of the scientific community to Browning's prediction. In our February 1991 survey, we asked people about their perception of scientists' response to the Browning prediction. Only half (50.3 percent) chose what can be described as the factually correct answer: "Scientists generally agreed that an earthquake was not likely." Almost as many, 41.3 percent, chose this response: "Scientists disagreed among themselves" about the prediction. Most of the rest, 7.0 percent, chose this response: "Scientists generally agreed that an earthquake was likely." Thus, many people may not have perceived Browning as opposing the scientific community, but rather as taking one side in a legitimate scientific debate. Moreover, those who saw scientists as divided among themselves over the Browning prediction were modestly more likely to believe Browning than those who saw scientists as rejecting Browning's prediction. Matching of respondents between the October and February surveys showed that more than 68 percent of those who saw scientists as divided had thought that a December quake was at least somewhat likely, compared with 57 percent of those who thought scientists had generally rejected the prediction. Moreover, 21.5 percent of the latter but only 12.5 percent of the former had said that a December quake was "very unlikely." Hence, the perception of a scientific dispute, more so than out-and-out distrust of science, may have helped give impetus to a widespread response to Browning.

In fact, the scientific community's reaction, albeit very slow to come, was clearly one of overwhelming rejection of Browning's prediction. As we noted in chapter 1, earthquake scientists at first paid little attention to the prediction, because they did not want to give it credibility by talking about it (Gori, 1993: 968). While some individual seismologists were contacted by the press and stated that Browning's prediction was not credible, there was no organized response by the scientific community until a panel of experts convened by the National Earthquake Prediction Evaluation Council (NEPEC) issued a statement on October 18, 1990, that there was no scientific basis for the prediction. This statement received considerable press attention, but by that time the cat was out of the bag—Browning's prediction had been the focus of heavy news media attention for more than six weeks. Nonetheless, since our question about scientists' response to Browning's prediction was asked after the prediction was disconfirmed, people who kept up with media reports should have understood that scientists rejected Browning's position. Not only had the prediction itself proven wrong but considerable media attention had also by then been given to the NEPEC statement and other scientific statements rejecting the prediction.

**The Effect of a Scientific Maverick: David Stewart**. Although we did not directly ask, it would appear that a series of statements by the one earthquake scientist who did partially support Browning, David Stewart, may have contributed to much of the confusion. At the time, Stewart was director of the Center for Earthquake Studies at Southeast Missouri State University. He helped to disseminate Browning's prediction by announcing it at a teachers' earthquake workshop in Arkansas in June 1990 (Gori, 1993: 967) and by calling it to the attention of audiences in Indiana and Missouri later that year (Spence et al., 1993). He also made statements that at least partially supported Browning's prediction and clearly supported the idea (later shown to be untrue) that Browning had correctly predicted past quakes. For example, he told the *Dallas Morning News*, "Here's a man who verifiably has hit several home runs, and he's up to bat. . . . You can't ignore the batting record"; and to the *New York Times*, he said, "Will he hit another on December 3? We don't know, but there's no excuse for not being prepared" (Spence et al., 1993: 10). Although Stewart was the only seismologist to even partially endorse Browning's prediction, his statements received wide media attention. According to Spence et al. (1993), he was quoted more often than Browning himself.

Our finding that half of our respondents did not perceive that scientists generally rejected the prediction is significant in the light of these events. Stewart was the only earthquake scientist who publicly supported Browning in even a limited way. But having just one scientist speaking positively of Browning's prediction enabled the news media to find and interview a scientist to take Browning's side, with the result that statements rejecting Browning's prediction were often juxtaposed with quotations or reports about Stewart's support of Browning. Our data support the notion that one scientist quoted in the media as taking a position rejected by the rest of the scientific community is all it takes to lead many people to perceive that scientists are divided on an issue. In fact, nearly half of our sample did perceive scientists as being divided about the Browning prediction. Hence, to many, Browning was seen not so much as opposing science as taking one side in a scientific debate—and taking a side that offered a certainty and precision that the perceived other side could not.

**Skepticism and Response to the Browning Prediction.** To assess more directly how people's views of science influenced their attitudes toward Browning, we asked respondents whether scientists were a "good," "fair," or "poor" source of information about earthquakes. To our initial surprise, those who responded "good" were more likely to believe Browning's prediction than those who said "fair" or especially "poor" (see table 2-6). This would appear unexpected, based on the aforementioned argument that part of Browning's attraction was a populist appeal to those who distrusted "big science." However, examination of other responses in table 2-6 suggests an explanation for our finding. This finding was not particular to science. We also asked people about government and business as sources of information about earthquakes and found a similar pattern. For all three sources—science, government, and business—people who said they were a "good" source of information were most likely to believe Browning, while those who said they were a "poor" source were least likely to do so, at least in St. Louis.

It would appear based on this finding that people who were trusting of one source of information would be trusting of others, including Browning. Those who distrusted one source distrusted others—again including Browning. In general, it appears that generalized skepticism—about any source of information—was negatively correlated with believing Browning, while trust or acceptance—again of any source of information—was positively correlated. This is consistent with our earlier discussions of the relationships of gender and education with believing Browning: Lower levels of education and the socially prescribed female gender role would be associated with lower levels of skepticism and, therefore, a greater tendency to believe Browning's prediction.

This finding is also consistent with findings of past studies introduced in chapter 1. In those studies, Turner, Nigg, and Paz (1986) found that people used scientific and nonscientific studies together to evaluate earthquake risk in Los Angeles in the mid-1970s; Mileti, Fitzpatrick, and Farhar (1990) found that people who thought that psychics could predict earthquakes were also more likely to believe a scientific prediction of an earthquake.

**Perceived Actions of Others.** In general, the responses of people's friends and of their employers were related to how seriously people took the prediction. The prediction was more widely believed by people whose friends and employers were planning to change their schedules. This is evident in table 2-6. In both the St. Louis area and Cape Girardeau/Sikeston, the percentage who considered a damaging December quake somewhat or very likely was highest among those who said most of their friends were planning schedule changes around December 2–3, lowest among those who said none of their friends were planning schedule changes, and intermediate among those who said some of their friends were planning schedule changes. In both St. Louis and Cape Girardeau/Sikeston, more than 80 percent of those who said that most of their friends were planning schedule changes also said they thought an earthquake was at least somewhat likely. In contrast, fewer than half of those in St. Louis who said that none of their friends were planning schedule changes thought a quake was at least somewhat likely. The difference was less, but still sizable, in Cape Girardeau/Sikeston. And in both regions, those who said that their employers were changing work schedules around the date of the predicted earthquake were much more likely than others to consider a December earthquake at least somewhat likely. These findings clearly show that those who perceived that others were reacting strongly to the prediction were much more likely to believe the prediction themselves. Moreover, we shall see shortly that as significant as the actions of others were in terms of whether people believed the prediction, they were an even more important factor in terms of what people planned to do about the prediction.

**Impact of the September Earthquake.** As noted above, a minor earthquake, magnitude 4.6, occurred on September 26, centered just west of Cape Girardeau. We wanted to see whether and how this event influenced people's perceptions about the Browning prediction. Our survey revealed that only 16 percent of respondents in the St. Louis area felt the September 26 earthquake, but nearly 80 percent in Cape Girardeau and about 67 percent in Sikeston felt the quake. About one-third of St. Louis area respondents said that this minor quake affected their thinking about the likelihood of a major quake in December, but in both Cape Girardeau and Sikeston, the majority of respondents said that this was the case.

Virtually all of the influence of the September 26 earthquake was to give greater credibility to Browning. Actually feeling the earthquake was only moderately correlated to believing the Browning prediction, but in all the areas we surveyed, those who said that their thinking was influenced by the September 26 earthquake thought that a December quake was more likely than those who said that their thinking was not influenced. Thus, among the sizable proportion who said that their thinking was affected by the September 26 earthquake, the effect was nearly always to make people more likely to believe the prediction. This is quite similar to the effects Turner, Nigg, and Paz (1986) found in the case of a similar minor earthquake during a period of heightened earthquake concern in Los Angeles.

### Thinking Versus Doing: The Two-Step Flow of Communication

Of course, what people thought about the Browning prediction and what they planned to do about it are two different things. It appears that the two-step flow of communication model developed by Lazarsfeld, Berelson, and Gaudet (1944; see also Katz, 1957) and applied to earthquake predictions and statements by Turner, Nigg, and Paz (1986) is particularly relevant to the question of what people plan to do and what they actually do in response to earthquake predictions. The two-step flow of communication model suggests that people receive their information from the mass media, but they evaluate the meaning of that information and decide what to do about it on the basis of discussions with and observations of actions taken by family, friends, and neighbors. In other words, after people get their initial information from the media, they develop a response to that information through interactions with significant others. Turner, Nigg, and Paz (1986) found that significant others had a strong influence over whether earthquake preparedness actions were taken. Mileti and Fitzpatrick (1991; 1993) found the same with respect to preparedness actions taken in response to the Parkfield Earthquake Prediction Experiment in California: When people saw their friends and neighbors taking actions to prepare for an earthquake, they were more likely to do so themselves. Baker (1979) found much the same with respect to evacuation behavior during hurricane warnings; a study of evacuation behavior by Mikami and Ikeda (1985) found similar effects of the actions of neighbors, family, and neighborhood organizations. The observed behavior of others has also been found to influence how people behave in situations of hysterical contagion (Kerckhoff, Back, and Miller, 1965) and collective behavior in crowds (Couch, 1970). We have already seen that people's belief in the prediction was correlated with what they believed their friends and employers were doing about the prediction. However, it turns out that these variables were even more important in explaining what people planned to do as a result of the prediction, much as the two-step flow of communication theory predicts.

**Correlates of Planning Schedule Changes for the Time of the Predicted Earthquake.** Table 2-7 shows cross-tabulations of various opinions and characteristics with whether or not respondents planned changes in their schedule around December 3, along with chi-square tests of significance for each cross-tabulation. Not surprisingly, people who thought that a major December quake was "very likely" or "somewhat likely" were more likely to plan schedule changes than people who thought such a quake was "not too likely" or "very unlikely." Significantly, however, many people who thought a quake likely did not plan schedule changes, and many who thought a quake unlikely did plan schedule changes. In fact, the relationship between the perceived likelihood of a major quake and planning schedule changes was not statistically significant in the Cape Girardeau/Sikeston areas. Thus, the perceived likelihood of a major quake was clearly not the only factor influencing what people planned to do, nor, in the Cape Girardeau and Sikeston areas, was it even an important influence.

In general, people with children under eighteen were more likely to plan changes than people without children. One interpretation is that such people planned changes to protect their children; another is that they had to change their schedules because of school closings in some areas. The latter, in fact, appears to be the more accurate interpretation. Among respondents who indicated that schools in their community were not changing their schedules, households with children were only slightly more likely than households without children to plan changes in their schedules. This may help to explain the fact that even some people who did not think a December quake very likely were planning to change their schedules. This issue will be explored further in multivariate analyses reported later in this chapter; however, the findings presented thus far suggest that the actions of institutions such as schools played an important role in determining people's plans for the period of the predicted earthquake.

Table 2-7. Percentage of Various Population Groups That Planned Changes in Their Schedules or the Schedules of Their Families Around December 3

| | St. Louis Area (%) | Cape Girardeau/ Sikeston Areas (%) |
|---|---|---|
| December quake very or somewhat likely | 36.2 | 54.3 |
| December quake not to likely or very unlikely | 14.9 | 43.6 |
| | $N = 319$   $Chi^2 = 16.70$ $df = 1$   $p < .0001$ | $N = 144$   $Chi^2 = 0.91$ $df = 1$   n.s. |
| Households with children under 18 | 36.2 | 61.8 |
| Households without children under 18 | 20.4 | 39.7 |
| | $N = 371$   $Chi^2 = 10.34$ $df = 1$   $p < .002$ | $N = 154$   $Chi^2 = 6.66$ $df = 1$   $p < .01$ |
| Most friends changing schedule | 74.5 | 75.0 |
| Some friends changing schedule | 34.3 | 32.9 |
| No friends changing schedule | 4.5 | 23.8 |
| | $N = 377$   $Chi^2 = 98.07$ $df = 2$   $p < .0001$ | $N = 159$   $Chi^2 = 30.99$ $df = 2$   $p < .0001$ |
| Employers changing schedule | 61.7 | 75.5 |
| Employers not changing schedule | 18.6 | 38.0 |
| | $N = 367$   $Chi^2 = 46.70$ $df = 1$   $p < .0001$ | $N = 153$   $Chi^2 = 17.99$ $df = 1$   $p < .0001$ |

Table 2-7 continued

| | | | | |
|---|---|---|---|---|
| Schools changing schedule | 48.0 | | 51.0 | |
| Schools not changing schedule | 16.1 | | 46.2 | |
| | $N = 317$   Chi$^2$ = 34.35 <br> df = 1   p < .0001 | | $N = 160$   Chi$^2$ = .002 <br> df = 1   n.s. | |
| Felt September quake | 26.2 | | 53.8 | |
| Did not feel September quake | 26.8 | | 36.6 | |
| | $N = 378$   Chi$^2$ = 0 <br> df = 1   n.s. | | $N = 160$   Chi$^2$ = 2.95 <br> df = 1   p < .09 | |
| September quake changed thinking | 37.9 | | 54.8 | |
| September quake did not change thinking | 21.1 | | 42.4 | |
| | $N = 370$   Chi$^2$ = 10.98 <br> df = 1   p < .0009 | | $N = 159$   Chi$^2$ = 1.91 <br> df = 1   p < .17 | |
| War with Iraq likely | 33.0 | | 51.9 | |
| War with Iraq not likely | 20.2 | | 53.7 | |
| | $N = 311$   Chi$^2$ = 5.57 <br> df = 1   p < .02 | | $N = 131$   Chi$^2$ = 0 <br> df = 1   n.s. | |

In addition to the effects of school closings, the perceived plans of friends and employers were also an important determinant of whether respondents planned changes in their own schedules. In fact, the best predictor of whether people planned to change their schedules (at least in the zero order) was whether, to the best of their knowledge, their friends planned to change their schedules. These findings strongly support the two-step flow of communication interpretation introduced above: What people see their friends and neighbors doing is a major influence over how seriously they take the forecast and, especially, what they plan to do about it. The actions of institutions such as schools and employers have a similar, though slightly smaller, effect, both by contributing to their sense of concern and by making schedule changes to which workers, students, and parents must adapt. (One exception is that respondents' self-reports about school schedule changes were not correlated significantly to planned schedule changes in the Cape Girardeau and Sikeston areas. The likely explanation for this is that virtually all schools in those areas were to be closed; there were almost no respondents whose community schools were to remain open.)

Those whose thinking was influenced by the September quake were also more likely to plan changes in their schedule for early December, but this difference was statistically significant only in the St. Louis area. Paradoxically, the opposite geographic pattern is true of the effect of feeling the September quake: People who felt the quake in Cape Girardeau and Sikeston were more likely to plan changes than the relatively few people who did not, but in the St. Louis area, there was no difference in planned changes between people who did and did not feel the quake.

*The International Situation and Earthquake Fears*

As noted in chapter 1, previous social science research has suggested that the public is particularly susceptible to fears and concerns about disaster during times of war or threat of war (Rose, 1982: 28–29; Beer, 1981: 56–57). Examples of mass hysteria arising partly or entirely from fears about war can be seen in the two incidents already cited that occurred during World War II: the "Great Los Angeles Air Raid," in which both the public and civil defense officials incorrectly believed that Los Angeles was under air attack by the Japanese (Mazon, 1984: 16–19), and the "War of the Worlds" incident, in which many (though fewer than widely believed) thought that a radio play about the earth's being invaded by Martians was real (Cantril, 1965; Rosengren et al., 1975). During the time in which the Browning prediction became well known, the United States was gearing up for a possible war with Iraq as a result of Iraq's invasion of Kuwait. We suspected that this situation might be a contributing factor to mass hysteria surrounding the Browning prediction.

To determine the effect of the threat of war on people's response to the Browning prediction, the survey included a question on whether people thought a war with Iraq was likely. About half of those answering the survey thought such a war was likely, and about one-third thought that it was not likely. The rest said that they did not know. In both the St. Louis area and the Cape Girardeau/Sikeston areas, people who thought a war with Iraq likely also were significantly more apt to think that a December earthquake was likely (see table 2-6).

This finding supports the notion that the prewar atmosphere in the Middle East may have contributed to the spread of fears about earthquakes in mid-America. Another interpretation of this finding is possible, however. Some research suggests that people with generalized fears may respond more strongly to risk of disaster (Lazarus, 1966). In other words, people who worry about one threat are more likely also to worry about other threats. It is not possible from the present research to determine which of these explanations is more applicable to the Browning event, but it is clear that there was a correlation between expecting a war and expecting an earthquake. In the St. Louis area but not in Cape Girardeau and Sikeston, the expectation of a war with Iraq also was associated with planning schedule changes around December 3 (see table 2-7).

*Multivariate Analyses: Explaining Response to the Browning Prediction*

Clearly, a number of social, background, and environmental influences were linked to believing the Browning forecast and to planning changes on the basis of the forecast. These were explored further through multivariate regression analyses, a method that allows examination of the relative influence of different predictor variables on the dependent variable. It also makes possible assessment of the proportion of variation in the dependent variable that can be explained by the combined effect of several predictor variables. The results of these analyses are reported in tables 2-8 and 2-9. Table 2-8 shows results of a series of regression analyses of the perceived likelihood of a major earthquake on or about December 3. These analyses were performed for the St. Louis area sample, a sample composed of the Cape Girardeau and Sikeston respondents, and a combined sample of all respondents in the survey. The *N* in these analyses is reduced somewhat from that of the cross-tabulations, because missing data on any variable included in the regression analyses results in a respondent's exclusion from the analysis—that is, missing cases must be excluded listwise rather than casewise. Zero order correlation matrices were generated and examined for possible correlations among predictor variables. Nearly all

Table 2-8. Regression Analysis of Perceived Likelihood of Earthquake on December 3

| Independent Variables | St. Louis Metropolitan Area $N = 216$ | | Cape Girardeau/ Sikeston Areas $N = 107$ | | Combined Areas $N = 323$ | |
|---|---|---|---|---|---|---|
| | B | Beta | B | Beta | B | Beta |
| *Group 1* | | | | | | |
| Education | -.178[a] | -.155 | -.114 | -.122 | -.157[b] | -.144 |
| Gender* | .298[a] | .144 | .405[a] | .225 | .322[c] | .160 |
| $R^2$ added, Group 1 | .077 | | .124 | | .083 | |
| Adusted $R^2$ added | .068 | | .107 | | .078 | |
| *Group 2* | | | | | | |
| Felt Sept. quake | .236 | .086 | .135 | .064 | .173 | .085 |
| Quake changed thinking | .386[b] | .184 | .256 | .177 | .340[c] | .172 |
| War likely | .242 | .118 | .196 | .110 | .223[a] | .112 |
| $R^2$ added, Group 2 | .071 | | .048 | | .089 | |
| Adusted $R^2$ added | .060 | | .024 | | .081 | |
| *Group 3* | | | | | | |
| School changes | .244 | .112 | .129 | .043 | .197 | .100 |
| Friends plan changes | .072 | .047 | .171 | .129 | .108 | .078 |
| $R^2/R^2$ added, Group 3 | .166/.018 | | .191/.019 | | .190/.018 | |
| Adusted $R^2$/added | .138/.010 | | .134/.003 | | .172/.013 | |
| F/Significance of Regression | 5.90/.0001 | | 3.34/.004 | | 9.27/.0001 | |

*Positive sign: Women more likely
[a] $p < .05$
[b] $p < .01$
[c] $p < .005$

such correlations were on the order of .35 or less, and in no case did they exceed approximately .6. Thus it is concluded that distortion of regression results due to multicolinearity was extremely unlikely to have occurred.

**Respondents' Perceptions of Earthquake Likelihood.** Table 2-8 presents results from a series of regression analyses of the perceived likelihood of a major earthquake on December 3. Education and gender, as demographic characteristics, were entered into the analysis first (Group 1 of variables) and together explained about 7 percent of the variance in St. Louis, 11 percent in Cape Girardeau and Sikeston, and 8 percent in the combined sample. (The proportion of the variance in perceived earthquake likelihood that is explained by the predictor variables in the model is indicated by the squared multiple regression coefficient, $R^2$. In the table, the explained variance added by each group of independent variables is shown in the lines labeled "$R^2$ Added." The coefficients shown in the table are based on the complete model with all predictor variables shown in the table included.) The coefficients of both education and gender are statistically significant, and their signs are the same as in the zero order relationships. However, as noted, they do not account for much variance. Entered next were perceptual/attitudinal variables: whether the respondent felt the September quake, whether the respondent's thinking was affected by that quake, and the perceived likelihood of war with Iraq (Group 2). These variables added 6 to 8 percentage points to $R^2$, but less in Cape Girardeau and Sikeston. Their signs are in the predicted direction and two of the three are statistically significant in the combined sample. However, in both St. Louis and the southeast Missouri (Cape Girardeau/Sikeston) sample, feeling the September quake had only minor and insignificant effects on the perceived likelihood of a December quake.

Added next to the analysis were perceptions regarding planned schedule changes on the part of friends and neighbors and of schools (Group 3). These predictor variables had nonsignificant coefficients and made little difference in $R^2$. Finally, in the combined sample only, the effect of location was assessed, using the variable zone to indicate whether the respondent lived in the St. Louis area or the Cape Girardeau/Sikeston areas. This variable was not statistically significant and added little to $R^2$, and it is not included in table 2-8.

In the combined sample, adjusted $R^2$ is .17. Education, gender, whether the September earthquake changed the respondent's thinking, and the respondent's perceived likelihood of war with Iraq all had significant effects upon the respondent's perceptions about the likelihood of a major earthquake on December 3. On the other hand, the actions of schools, friends, and neighbors appeared to have had little effect on the respondents' perceptions about the likelihood of a major earthquake.[*] As we turn next to an analysis of what respondents planned to do, however, we will find a very different pattern.

**Respondent's Plans for Schedule Changes.** Table 2-9 shows the results from a similar series of regression analyses of whether respondents planned schedule changes around December 3. We begin by examining the effect of respondents' belief in the likelihood of a major December quake. The effect is surprisingly small—although people who thought a quake likely were more likely to plan schedule changes, the perceived likelihood of a quake accounted for only 5 percent of the variance in planned schedule changes in St. Louis, only 4 percent in the combined sample, and virtually none at all in Cape Girardeau and Sikeston. Thus, as was suggested earlier, other factors had a bigger impact on what people actually planned to do. The effects of demographic factors—primarily whether respondents had children—were somewhat greater. Addition of this variable, along with gender and education, increased adjusted $R^2$ to about .08 in St. Louis and the combined sample, but only to .035 in Cape Girardeau and Sikeston (Group 2). Of the three new variables, only the presence of children had a statistically significant coefficient. In contrast to their effect on believing the forecast, education and gender had no important effects on whether respondents planned schedule changes in response to the earthquake forecast.

Group 3 predictors include perceptual/attitudinal variables: whether the respondents felt the September quake, whether the quake changed their thinking about the likelihood of a major December quake, and the perceived likelihood of war with Iraq. Again, these variables had nonsignificant effects and added little to $R^2$. Group 4 predictors add the perceived response of friends

*We also conducted a variety of other regression analyses and cross-tabulations not reported in detail here. These revealed that believing the Browning prediction was uncorrelated to the number of sources from which people had heard about the prediction, whether they had discussed the prediction among themselves, and perceptions about what Browning's occupation was.

Table 2-9. Regression Analysis of Planned Changes in Schedule

| Independent Variables | St. Louis Metropolitan Area $N = 216$ | | Cape Girardeau/ Sikeston Areas $N = 107$ | | Combined Areas $N = 323$ | |
|---|---|---|---|---|---|---|
| | B | Beta | B | Beta | B | Beta |
| *Group 1* | | | | | | |
| Quake likely on December 3? | .045 | .098 | -.001 | -.001 | .033 | .067 |
| $R^2$ added | .058 | | .004 | | .047 | |
| Adusted $R^2$ added | .053 | | 0 | | .044 | |
| | | | | | | |
| *Group 2* | | | | | | |
| Education | .021 | .040 | .001 | .001 | .001 | .015 |
| Gender* | .049 | .051 | -.067 | -.066 | .000 | .000 |
| Children | .139[a] | .151 | .179[a] | .180 | .139[c] | .143 |
| $R^2$ added, Group 2 | .042 | | .069 | | .050 | |
| Adusted $R^2$ added | .028 | | .035 | | .040 | |
| | | | | | | |
| *Group 3* | | | | | | |
| Felt quake | .072 | .057 | .165 | .139 | .066 | .066 |
| Quake changed thinking | .043 | .045 | -.000 | -.000 | .016 | .016 |
| War likely | .066 | .070 | -.062 | -.061 | .014 | .014 |
| $R^2$ added, Group 3 | .028 | | .034 | | .044 | |
| Adusted $R^2$ added | .015 | | .006 | | .037 | |
| | | | | | | |
| *Group 4* | | | | | | |
| School changes | .177[b] | .177 | -.288 | -.172 | .065 | .067 |
| Work changes | .177[a] | .146 | .321[d] | .306 | .244[d] | .212 |
| Friends plan changes | .216[d] | .313 | .287[d] | .385 | .246[d] | .359 |
| $R^2/R^2$ added, Group 4 | .347/.219 | | .375/.268 | | .360/.219 | |
| Adjusted $R^2$/added, Group 4 | .313/.217 | | .307/.266 | | .338/.218 | |
| | | | | | | |
| F | 10.00 | | 5.52 | | 16.39 | |
| Significance of Regression | .0001 | | .0001 | | .0001 | |

*Positive sign for gender indicates that women more likely to plan changes.

[a] $p < .05$

[b] $p < .01$

[c] $p < .005$

[d] $p < .001$

*57*

and neighbors, employers, and schools to the analysis, and those turn out to be the variables that have major effects on respondents' plans. In all three samples, $R^2$ increased by more than .2 with the addition of these variables, and adjusted $R^2$ with these variables included exceeds .30 in all of the samples. In other words, these three variables by themselves explain more than 20 percent of the variance in planned schedule changes. Thus, the perceived responses of significant others and of institutions clearly had a major impact on what respondents planned to do on December 3.

The relative influence of different predictor variables can be assessed by comparing their beta coefficients (standardized regression coefficients). Such comparison clearly shows that the variable most strongly related to what people planned to do on December 3 was their own perception about their friends' and neighbors' plans to change their schedules. In all three geographic samples, this variable easily had the highest beta coefficient, indicating that it had the largest effect on whether people planned to change their own schedules. To put this slightly differently, the best predictor of whether people planned to change their schedules was whether they thought their friends and neighbors were changing their schedules. This suggests strongly that interpersonal processes and behavioral modeling, not schedule changes forced by the actions of institutions, were the most important single force shaping people's planned response to the earthquake forecast. This provides strong support for the two-step flow of communication interpretation discussed above. In addition, it is clear that this effect applies mainly to what people planned to do, since the perceived plans of friends and neighbors had little effect on whether respondents thought that a December earthquake was likely.

Institutions also made a difference in what people planned, and that was particularly true for the actions of employers, whose beta coefficients were larger in the combined sample than those of schools. Schools appear to have made a difference mainly in the St. Louis area, where about 25 percent of respondents reported that schools were changing their schedules. They made less difference in variation within the Cape Girardeau/Sikeston sample, where there were few respondents whose schools were not closed. Interestingly, in this area, the coefficient for schools was the opposite of what would be expected; perhaps this was a distortion resulting from the very small number of respondents whose schools were not closed. Finally, in a regression analysis not reported here, we found that location—Cape Girardeau/Sikeston versus the St. Louis area—had no effect on planned schedule changes. That is remarkable in light of the fact that in the zero order, southeast Missouri residents were much more likely than St. Louis area residents to plan schedule changes. It indicates that this difference is entirely attributable to differences between these areas in the perceived behavioral response of significant others and of institutions to the earthquake forecast.

## Summary and Conclusions

In this chapter, we have seen that a sizable minority of the population believed Iben Browning's earthquake prediction, and that only a minority of the population clearly rejected it. The bulk of the population fell somewhere in the middle, neither clearly believing nor clearly rejecting the prediction. It appears that a somewhat larger proportion of the population than in earlier pseudo-disaster situations was caught up to some degree in the Browning prediction, although the proportion may have been similar in the one incident most similar to the Browning prediction, Henry Minturn's pseudoscientific prediction of an earthquake in Los Angeles in 1976.

It is clear that believing the prediction and planning to do something about it, though modestly correlated, were two very different things. Believing the prediction was a poor predictor of plans to take action to protect oneself and one's family on December 3, and the factors influencing beliefs and action plans were quite different. The main factors influencing people's beliefs about the likelihood that Browning's prediction would come true were their educational level, their gender, their perceptions about the significance of the minor earthquake on September 26, and their expectations of a war with Iraq. Underlying these correlations were the effects of people's degree of skepticism, and probably their tendency toward generalized worry about risk. Key factors contributing to belief in Browning's prediction would appear to have been the media's initial uncritical acceptance of Browning's claims to have predicted past earthquakes, and confusion about the response of science to the Browning prediction—many saw scientists as divided among themselves about the prediction. This perception was probably enhanced by David Stewart's widely quoted statements supporting Browning, and the news media's widespread reporting of Stewart as a scientist who supported Browning.

As suggested by the two-step flow of communication theory, the factors influencing what people planned to do about the Browning prediction were quite different: They hinged largely on what they perceived their friends and neighbors to be doing. Institutional responses also made some difference, though not as much, in what people planned to do. Of course, what they planned to do in October and what they actually did in December were not always the same—in fact, they often were not. In chapter 3, we turn to an analysis of what people actually did, the determinants of what they did, and how what they did compared with what they had said they were going to do.

# 3

# What They Did Compared with
# What They Planned

IT IS, OF COURSE, one thing to say six weeks before the date of a predicted earthquake that you plan to leave town or stay home from work, and another thing actually to do it. This is one reason we decided from the start to do a follow-up survey of as many of the October respondents as we could the following February. We were also interested in finding out whether any heightened awareness of earthquake risk and any preparedness actions people might have taken before the date of the predicted earthquake would still be in place after the date had passed. A common joke in the St. Louis area was that the sewers would be flooded on December 4, when residents dumped their bottled water. We did not think it likely that all would dump their bottled water, but we were concerned about a possible "cry wolf" effect: When the predicted earthquake did not occur, would people incorrectly conclude that the entire idea of earthquake risk in mid-America was false, something they no longer needed to worry about or prepare for?

## Planned Versus Actual Changes in Schedule

We turn our attention first to actions specifically taken by respondents to protect themselves from an earthquake at the time predicted by Browning. To measure such actions, we focused on schedule changes, planned and (in our February survey) actual, at the time of the predicted earthquake. These included keeping children home from school, staying home from work, and leaving the area. As discussed in chapter 2, we found in our October survey that there was only a weak link between the cognitive dimension—that is, believing the Browning forecast—and the intended behavioral dimension—that is, planning schedule changes. In fact, what relationship there was almost entirely disappeared after controls for the responses of significant others and of schools and employers. We felt that the link between what people said in October that they planned to do and what they reported in February that they had actually done might also be weak.

Social research tells us that the intended behavioral dimension does not necessarily translate into actual behavior. People often can and do behave differently than they say they intend to or would, as was first illustrated by La Piere's classic study (1934). This is especially the case when, as in La Piere's study, there are costs of some type associated with carrying out the intended behavior. In the case of that study, people who at another time had stated an intention or policy of discriminating against Chinese Americans did not do so when confronted with a white man and a Chinese man traveling together and requesting services at their establishment. A major reason they did not is that there were costs—embarrassment, social pressure, and censure by the person of their own race, whose presence they probably had not anticipated when answering an abstract survey question. Faced with these costs, they did not discriminate.

Similarly, there were costs involved in changing one's schedule to avoid the predicted earthquake. School children and employees faced possible penalties or the risk of falling behind on work if they stayed home. People who left town would face these costs, plus the additional cost of travel. And everyone who stayed home from work or school or left town because of the earthquake scare faced possible ridicule if it did not happen. For these reasons, we were very interested in finding out three things in the February survey: (1) What proportion of those who said that they planned to change their schedule actually did? (2) What was the relationship between people saying that they planned to change their schedules (in the October survey) and actually changing them (as self-reported in the February survey)? (3) Was there any relationship between believing the forecast (as reported in October) and actually changing one's schedule (as reported in February)?

*Actual Schedule Changes*

Respondents to the February survey were asked specifically about three kinds of schedule changes: whether the respondent or any household member stayed home from work, whether any of the respondent's children were kept home from school, and whether anyone in the respondent's household left the area. Regarding the latter, respondents were offered choices of reporting that they had left because of the earthquake prediction or that they had left for other reasons. We knew that some people would be engaging in routine travel and we were interested only in people who left because of the earthquake prediction. These data are presented in table 3-1. Because of the smaller sample, most of the data reported from the February survey are from a combined St. Louis/Cape Girardeau/Sikeston sample. This methodology has the effect of somewhat overrepresenting people from the Cape Girardeau and especially Sikeston areas, but the advantage gained in terms of reliability was deemed worth the loss in representativeness. Without combining the sample, the Cape Girardeau and Sikeston samples would be unacceptably low, at 42 and 49 respectively. The total February sample was 293, including 202 from the St. Louis metropolitan area.

Table 3-1 shows the proportion who said in October that they planned to change their schedules around December 3 and the proportion who said in February that they actually did either keep their children home from school or stay home from work. For comparison purposes, the October data are shown for the full October sample, "constant households" (households that were interviewed in both the October and February surveys) and "constant individuals" (individuals who were interviewed in both October and February). The "full sample" respondents are included because the larger sample size offers greater reliability; the similarity of their responses to those of the constant individuals and constant households supports the interpretation that these smaller samples were quite similar to the larger ones. In the February sample, the data are shown for the whole sample ("constant households," which one had to be in order to be included in the sample, since only households that had been interviewed in October were called in February) as well as for constant individuals.

Table 3-1 shows that the proportion who said in February that they either kept their children home from school or stayed home from work was significantly lower than the proportion who had indicated in October that they planned schedule changes in response to the earthquake. For example, while 27.5 percent of constant individuals said in October that they planned schedule changes, only 15 percent of them reported in February that they had kept

Table 3-1. Percentage That Planned Schedule Changes (October 1990) and
Reported Actual Schedule Changes (February 1991)

|  | Full Sample | | Constant Households | | Constant Individuals | |
| --- | --- | --- | --- | --- | --- | --- |
|  | Yes (%) | No (%) | Yes (%) | No (%) | Yes (%) | No (%) |
| Planned schedule changes, October | 32.2 | 65.4[a] | 31.0 | 66.2 | 27.5 | 69.5 |
| N | 533 | | 284 | | 200 | |
| Kept children home from school, February survey | n.a. | | 17.2 | 82.7 | 15.0 | 85.0 |
| N | | | 191[b] | | 140[b] | |
| Stayed home from work, February survey | n.a. | | 9.1 | 89.9 | 8.2 | 91.8 |
| N | | | 290 | | 201 | |
| Planned to leave area, October | 6.5 | 92.4 | 7.8 | 89.7 | 5.6 | 93.5 |
| N | 560 | | 284 | | 200 | |
| Left area because of quake prediction, February survey | n.a. | | 1.0 | | 1.0 | |
| Left area for other reasons | n.a. | | 1.0 | | 1.0 | |
| Did not leave area | n.a. | | 97.9 | | 98.0 | |
| N | | | 287 | | 201 | |

[a]Where totals do not add to 100, the remainder responded "don't know."
[b]This item includes only respondents with school-age children.

children home from school, and only about 8 percent reported having stayed home from work. Leaving the area was even less common. Although 2 percent of our February respondents said they had left the area around December 3, only half of these—1 percent of the total sample—said that they had left because of the earthquake. Although that is a very small percentage, it is not an insignificant number of people. For example, if 1 percent of the population of the St. Louis area had left town because of the earthquake, that would have amounted to around twenty-five thousand people. Still, this was a small fraction of even the relatively small proportion of people who had said in October that they planned to leave the area. Around 6 percent had said in October that they planed to leave; only one out of six of those said in February that they actually had.

Moreover, among those that did make changes in their schedule short of leaving the area, many clearly did so because they had to adjust to schedule changes made by employers or, more likely, schools. Of the February respondents, 6.8 percent indicated that their work or the work of someone in their household had been canceled because of the earthquake forecast, and 23.6 percent of those who had school-age children said that their children's school had been canceled. If adjustment is made for these institutionally imposed schedule changes, we find that relatively few people changed their schedules on their own. For example, only 1.7 percent of people who had children and whose schools did not close reported keeping their children home. A slightly larger number, 5.5 percent, stayed home from work when work was not canceled. However, many of them did so to take care of children whose school had been canceled. Based on these findings, it is virtually certain that the actual behavioral response to the earthquake forecast was smaller in magnitude than the intended response measured in October, although the extent to which that is the case is uncertain for reasons we turn to next.

### The Question of Dissonance: Prospective Plans Versus Retrospective Self-Reports

There is, of course, another possible explanation for the discrepancy between what people said in October that they planned to do and what they said in February that they had actually done. It may be that people did in fact change their schedules, but, placed in a situation of cognitive dissonance when they had planned for an earthquake that did not happen, they do not now want to look or feel foolish by admitting that they changed their schedule. That would, of course, lead to some understatement of the actual response when people answered the February survey. We have no direct way of measuring this, but two items of information we obtained suggest that it may be the case. First, we asked them retrospectively in February how concerned they had been about the risk of an earthquake in December, offering them a set of four responses ranging from "very concerned" to "not at all concerned." Table 3-2 shows the frequency distribution for this February item and compares it with the frequency distribution for the item relating to the likelihood of a December quake from the October survey.

Table 3-2. Frequency Distributions, of Perceived Likelihood of a Quake (October 1990 Survey) and Self-Reported Concern Before December 3 (February 1991 Survey)

| | Perceived Likelihood of Quake | | | Self-Reported Concern Before December 3 | | |
| | Full Sample (%) | Constant Households (%) | Constant Individuals (%) | | Constant Households (%) | Constant Individuals (%) |
|---|---|---|---|---|---|---|
| Very likely | 17.6 | 12.8 | 12.0 | Very concerned | 9.9 | 10.9 |
| Somewhat likely | 38.6 | 44.3 | 44.8 | Somewhat concerned | 26.7 | 25.7 |
| Not too likely | 17.3 | 18.6 | 16.1 | Only a little | 32.3 | 30.7 |
| Very unlikely | 16.1 | 15.3 | 17.2 | Not at all | 28.8 | 30.2 |
| Don't know | 10.3 | 9.1 | 9.9 | Don't know | 2.4 | 0.0 |
| N | 533 | 274 | 203 | | 288 | 203 |

Some caution must be used in considering this comparison a test of dissonance effects. Research has shown that being concerned about the risk of an earthquake is clearly not the same as believing one is going to happen (Turner, Nigg, and Paz, 1986). Our own later surveys in 1992 and 1993 confirmed this: Those surveys included items measuring both concern and perceived likelihood of a quake, and the correlations between the two were often modest. Having noted this caveat, however, it is nonetheless striking that there is a sizable difference between the October measure for likelihood of a quake and the February measure of retrospective concern. In October, around 55–57 percent of the total sample thought that a quake was very or somewhat likely, but, in February, only around 37 percent of respondents said that they were very or somewhat concerned about that risk. In fact, as shown by the cross-tabulation in table 3-3, only slightly more than half of those who had thought a December quake very or somewhat likely in October reported in February that they had been very or somewhat concerned.

Table 3-3. Retrospective Self-Reported Concern (February 1991) by Perceived
Likelihood of December Quake (October 1990)

| Retrospective Self-Reported Concern | Perceived Likelihood of a Quake | | | |
| --- | --- | --- | --- | --- |
| | Very Likely (%) | Somewhat Likely (%) | Not Too Likely (%) | Not at All Likely (%) |
| Very concerned | 24.2 | 10.3 | 2.0 | 2.4 |
| Somewhat concerned | 33.3 | 33.3 | 20.0 | 14.6 |
| Only a little concerned | 24.2 | 34.2 | 52.0 | 22.0 |
| Not at all concerned | 18.2 | 22.2 | 26.0 | 61.0 |

$N = 241$    $Chi^2 = 43.681$    $df = 9$    $p < .0001$

This finding by itself does not prove dissonance reduction, since there are
clearly reasons why a person could expect a quake but not be concerned about
it, such as believing that one's home and workplace are structurally safe from
earthquakes. This is a major reason why likelihood and concern measures are
often only modestly correlated. However, another item also suggests some dissonance reduction. Table 3-4 shows people's expectations of an earthquake in
the next ten or fifteen years, measured by identical items in October and February. It shows a 12–15 point decline in the percentage who thought such a
quake "very likely," coupled with a smaller increase in the "somewhat likely"
response. Taking the two categories together, this table shows a decrease from
about 85 percent in October to about 74 percent in February in the percentage who thought such a quake either "very likely" or "somewhat likely." In
other words, there was, for at least some people, a decline in the belief that the
area is at long-range risk for a damaging earthquake. That, of course, indicates
an attitude shift, but it does not by itself suggest dissonance reduction. However, what does suggest dissonance reduction is that people will not admit to
such an opinion shift.

As shown in table 3-5, we asked our February respondents whether there
had been any change in their thinking about earthquake risk within the next
ten or fifteen years, since before the predicted date of the quake. A clear majority said that there had not been, and among those who said that their opinion had changed, more said they now thought there was a greater risk than the

Table 3-4. Perceived Likelihood of a Quake Within the Next Ten or Fifteen Years (October 1990 and February 1991)

|  | October 1990 | | | February 1991 | |
| --- | --- | --- | --- | --- | --- |
|  | Full Sample (%) | Constant Households (%) | Constant Individuals (%) | All February Respondents (%) | Constant Individuals (%) |
| Very likely | 51.0 | 51.4 | 50.5 | 34.6 | 38.8 |
| Somewhat likely | 34.9 | 35.6 | 35.6 | 49.8 | 45.3 |
| Not too likely | 5.5 | 5.5 | 5.4 | 9.3 | 9.0 |
| Very unlikely | 3.6 | 3.4 | 4.0 | 3.8 | 4.5 |
| Don't know | 5.0 | 4.1 | 4.5 | 2.4 | 2.5 |
| N | 582 | 292 | 202 | 289 | 201 |

other way around. The problem is, of course, that the shift in their actual responses on the likelihood of such a quake was in the opposite direction. In other words, there appears to have been, in a number of cases, an unacknowledged change of opinion, suggesting that at least some people had thought the long-term risk of a quake was greater before December 3, but they did not want to admit to such an attitude change because that might be tacitly admitting that they had believed Browning's forecast.

Finally, the survey results can be compared with other indicators of similar behavior. We found that less than 2 percent of our respondents with children whose schools were open reported having kept their children home. However, in some parts of the St. Louis metropolitan area, school attendance ran only around two-thirds of normal on December 3 (Uhlenbrock, 1990). Allowing for normal absences, this suggests that unusual absences may have reached around 25 percent of enrollment in these districts. Other districts, however, had no increases in absence. Nonetheless, these school attendance data suggest at least a somewhat higher absence rate than implied by our survey data, which is consistent with the idea that some may have reduced dissonance by understating their behavioral response to the earthquake.

In summary, it is virtually certain that fewer people changed their schedules than said they intended to make changes. That was particularly true for

Table 3-5. Self-Reported Changes in Perceived Likelihood of a Quake and in Concern about Quakes (February 1991)

| Perceived Likelihood of a Quake Within Next Ten to Fifteen Years Compared with Belief Before December 3 | | | | Concern about Earthquake Now Compared with Concern Before December 3 | | |
|---|---|---|---|---|---|---|
| | All February Respondents (%) | Constant Individuals (%) | | | All February Respondents (%) | Constant Individuals (%) |
| Now think quake more likely | 21.1 | 17.6 | | Now more concerned | 15.8 | 12.1 |
| No change | 62.1 | 65.3 | | No change | 71.9 | 75.2 |
| Now think quake less likely | 14.4 | 15.6 | | Now less concerned | 10.9 | 12.1 |
| Don't know | 2.4 | 1.5 | | Don't know | 1.4 | 0.5 |

changes not mandated by work or school closures. On the other hand, we do not clearly know how many fewer, since part of the apparent difference may reflect people reducing their dissonance after the quake failed to occur by denying actions that they had taken. Thus, the true figures are probably higher than the February responses suggest. At the same time, they are almost certainly lower than what people's intentions in October would have implied.

*October Earthquake Attitudes and Plans and Self-Reported Schedule Changes*

On the one hand, institutional changes were clearly a major factor—and perhaps the major factor—in actual self-reported schedule changes as measured in February. On the other hand, there were some clear relationships between self-reported schedule changes in February and October data concerning the likelihood of a quake and plans to make schedule changes. As shown in table 3-6, there was a strong and statistically significant relationship between perceptions of the likelihood of a quake as reported in October and self-reports in February of having kept children home from school. In fact, the percentage who reported in February that they had kept their children home was ten times greater among those who had said in October that a December quake was "very likely" than among those who had said that it was "very unlikely."

There was a weaker relationship, just missing .05 statistical significance, between believing in October that a December quake was likely and self-reports made in February of having stayed home from work because of the risk. As shown in table 3-6, there was also a strong and statistically significant relationship between having said in October that one planned schedule changes and reporting in February that one's children had been kept home from school or that someone in the household had stayed home. In fact, those who had said in October that they planned schedule changes were three to four times more likely to have reported making schedule changes in the follow-up survey. Still, it is true that only a rather small minority of even those who had indicated plans for schedule changes actually reported in the later survey that they stayed home from work (about 19 percent) or kept children home from school (about 29 percent).

Finally, a similar relationship was found between beliefs in October about the likelihood of a December quake and retrospective reports in February of concern about such a quake. In general, as shown by table 3-3, the more likely people said in October that a December quake was, the more they reported in February that they had been concerned about such a quake. This is one of the strongest and most statistically significant relationships we observed in our comparison of the October and February data. Having said this, it is also important to reiterate that retrospective concern was measured at a notably lower level than pre-December expectations about the likelihood of a quake. Among those who had thought a December quake "very likely," for example, more than 42 percent reported having been "only a little concerned" or "not at all concerned." On the other hand, nearly everyone who had thought a quake unlikely in the October survey reported in February that they had been only a little or not at all concerned.

*Sociodemographics and Schedule Changes*

Our survey found that people with children were more likely to stay home from work than people with no children, and women were more likely to stay home from work than men (see table 3-7). Both of these findings may be attributable to people staying home to take care of children whose school was not in session; past research has shown, for example, that in families in which both parents work outside the home, it continues most often to be the wife and mother who misses work for reasons of child care (see Coverman and

Table 3-6. Self-Reported Schedule Changes (Unadjusted for Work or School Closures, from February 1991 Survey) by Perceived Likelihood of a Quake (from October 1990 Survey)

| | Percentage of Households That Kept a Child Home from School* | Percentage of Households in Which Someone Stayed Home from Work |
|---|---|---|
| **Perceived quake likelihood** | | |
| Very likely | 35.0 | 20.0 |
| Somewhat likely | 18.8 | 10.4 |
| Not too likely | 16.7 | 6.3 |
| Very unlikely | 3.2 | 2.6 |
| | $N = 167$ | $N = 237$ |
| | $\text{Chi}^2 = 8.772 \quad df = 3$ | $\text{Chi}^2 = 7.227 \quad df = 3$ |
| | $p < .04$ | $p < .06$ |
| | | |
| **Planned schedule changes?** | | |
| Yes | 29.3 | 19.3 |
| No | 12.0 | 4.5 |
| | $N = 175$ | $N = 259$ |
| | $\text{Chi}^2 = 6.857 \quad df = 1$ | $\text{Chi}^2 = 12.859 \quad df = 1$ |
| | $p < .009$ | $p < .0003$ |

*Includes only households with school age children.

Sheley, 1986; Hochschild, 1989). The data suggest a possible relationship between high educational levels and both keeping children home from school and staying home from work; however, the relationship is not statistically significant, so we cannot say with certainty that education is correlated with either. Finally, it might be noted that whites appear to have been more likely to stay home from work than blacks; again, the reason for this pattern may lie in the need to take care of children whose school was canceled; nearly all the blacks in the sample were in the St. Louis area, where schools were generally not canceled.

Table 3-7. Self-Reported Schedule Changes (Unadjusted for Work or School Closures, from February 1991 Survey) by Sociodemographics (from October 1990 Survey)

| Sociodemographic Variables | Percentage of Households That Kept a Child Home from School* | Percentage of Households in Which Someone Stayed Home from Work |
|---|---|---|
| **Race** | | |
| White | 19.3 | 10.1 |
| Black | 0.0 | 0.0 |
| | $N = 179$ | $N = 260$ |
| | $Chi^2 = 1.880$ $df = 1$ | $Chi^2 = 1.389$ $df = 1$ |
| | n.s. | n.s. |
| **Presence of children under 18** | | |
| None | n.a. | 4.7 |
| One or More | | 14.9 |
| | | $N = 262$ |
| | | $Chi^2 = 6.847$ $df = 1$ |
| | | $p < .009$ |
| **Education** | | |
| Less than 4 years high school | 28.6 | 11.1 |
| 4 years high school | 20.4 | 10.4 |
| Some college | 17.7 | 12.5 |
| 4 years college or more | 10.9 | 4.5 |
| | $N = 180$ | $N = 261$ |
| | $Chi^2 = 3.163$ $df = 3$ | $Chi^2 = 3.635$ $df = 3$ |
| | n.s. | n.s. |
| **Gender** | | |
| Female | 16.7 | 11.2 |
| Male | 18.7 | 5.8 |
| | $N = 189$ | $N = 272$ |
| | $Chi^2 = 0.025$ $df = 1$ | $Chi^2 = 1.648$ $df = 1$ |
| | n.s. | n.s. |

*Includes only households with school age children.

## Preparations for a Damaging Earthquake

### Rational Preparedness Versus Irrational Response

As the above findings show, some people responded to the Browning prediction in ways that earthquake scientists and disaster planners would regard as
irrational, such as planning to change schedules or leave town on the day on
which Browning predicted that an earthquake would occur. Although on a
percentage basis only a small minority of people actually did any of those
things, the absolute number who did so was sizable. When applied to the area's
actual population, the percentages in our survey imply that up to two hundred thousand people stayed home from work, and more kept their children
home from school. As noted above, the number who apparently left town on
the day of the predicted quake is much smaller, but it is still in the tens of thou-
sands. From the viewpoint of earthquake scientists and disaster planners,
those actions are irrational, in that existing scientific knowledge does not per-
mit the prediction of an earthquake on a given day. Such behaviors do nothing to protect people from the real, but time-uncertain, risk of a damaging
earthquake in the New Madrid Seismic Zone.

In fairness to individuals who acted irrationally, it is important to stress that
many institutions acted equally irrationally, a fact that clearly played a role
in shaping many individuals' behavior. These institutional actions included
closing schools on the day of the predicted earthquake, as was done throughout most of southeast Missouri including Cape Girardeau (Bliss, 1990), which
resulted in the cancellation of classes for forty thousand students in Missouri
alone (Pesce, 1990). Other examples included parking fire trucks outside of
fire stations on the predicted day of the earthquake to prevent damage should
the stations collapse, as was done in several St. Louis communities (Byrne,
1990). Emergency resources were mobilized for disaster drills or earthquake
exercises on the day of the predicted quake by the state of Arkansas (Gori,
1993) and several municipalities and counties (Byrne, 1990), and the national
guard was placed on standby in the states of Kentucky (Pesce, 1990) and Missouri (Landa, 1990). Private institutions as well as governments engaged in
such behavior. For example, the U.S. Figure Skating Association postponed a
regional competition that had been scheduled for St. Louis on December 3
(Allen and Gross, 1990).

It is also important to stress that the institutional and individual behaviors were mutually reinforcing. Seeing institutions such as schools and employers changing their schedules led many to plan their own schedule changes, as was noted in chapter 2—though fewer actually did change their schedules unless forced to do so by school or work cancellations. At the same time, however, the actions of individuals influenced actions taken by institutions. The most common reason given for closing schools, for example, was that if schools were open, attendance would be low, and the schools would lose state dollars appropriated on the basis of the number of students actually attending. This concern was not entirely unfounded: As we saw, school attendance was down somewhat in St. Louis; in some small towns in northeast Arkansas that kept their schools open, attendance was less than 50 percent on December 3 (Gordon, 1990). Similarly, the reason given for cancellation of the ice skating competition in St. Louis was that the cancellation was demanded by the parents of the children participating in the competition (Allen and Gross, 1990).

Whether individuals planned to change their schedules because of institutions, or institutions did so because of pressures generated by individuals, the fact is that the actions taken had little or no protective value because of the impossibility of predicting when an earthquake will occur. However, other actions taken by individuals and institutions in response to the Browning prediction may well have been helpful in terms of protecting themselves from the damaging earthquake that is certain to occur in the New Madrid Seismic Zone at some point in the future. The probabilities of an earthquake of around magnitude 6.0 or greater in the New Madrid region by the year 2000 have been placed at anywhere from 13 to 60 percent. Johnston and Nava (1985) placed the probability of a quake of magnitude 6.3 or greater during this time at 40–63 percent; Nishenko and Bollinger (1990), using a different methodology, estimated the chance of a quake of magnitude 6.0 by 2000 at 13 percent. The probability of such a quake by the year 2040—within the lifetime of most people now living in the region—has been placed at between 50 and 90 percent, with Nishenko and Bollinger arguing the lower figure and Johnston and Nava the higher one. The possibilities of a larger quake during the next fifty years or so are significantly smaller, and the chance of a repeat of the 1811–12 great quakes with magnitudes of up to 8.3 is minuscule during the next fifty years.

Nonetheless, a quake in the range of 6.0 to 6.5 is capable of causing significant damage, particularly to unreinforced masonry structures and to structures on unstable soils, such as the Mississippi River flood plain. Risk maps produced by the U.S. Geological survey show, for example, that in a magnitude 6.7 New Madrid earthquake, much of the St. Louis area would be in an area where walking and standing would be difficult, loose bricks would fall from buildings, windows would break, heavy furniture would be overturned, and some buildings would be damaged (Spence et al., 1993: 213). Clearly, damage and injury could be mitigated in such a situation if people took certain preparatory actions, such as knowing what to do, fastening objects that could fall, reinforcing weak structures, and storing supplies to weather the inevitable power outages. In parts of southeast Missouri and northwest Tennessee, the damage from a magnitude 6.7 quake would be even greater, including the partial collapse of some buildings and serious damage to most, houses shaken off their foundations, and the opening of cracks in the ground. In those areas, the potential benefits of preparation are even greater.

*Four Actions to Take to Prepare for a Damaging Earthquake*

To assess the extent to which the Browning prediction led people to take reasonable actions to prepare for a damaging quake, we asked respondents identical questions in the October and February surveys about four such actions. We asked them whether they had secured objects that could fall during an earthquake, whether they had stored food and water, whether they knew how to shut off their utilities, and whether they had earthquake insurance. Table 3-8 shows the October responses to these questions separately for the St. Louis area sample and for a combined Cape Girardeau-Sikeston sample.

**Preparedness in October 1990**. The data in table 3-8 show that, by the time of the October survey, the majority of respondents in both the St. Louis area and Cape Girardeau/Sikeston knew how to shut off their utilities, and the majority had earthquake insurance. More than half in Cape Girardeau and Sikeston had stored food and water; just over one-third of St. Louis area respondents had taken this step. The only one of these actions that had not been so widely taken was fastening objects that could fall: Only about one in three had done this in Cape Girardeau and Sikeston, and fewer than one in seven in the St. Louis area. This is consistent with findings from other surveys showing that the ease of taking a protective action is a major factor in the likeli-

Table 3-8. Level of Preparedness by Area (October 1990)

| | St. Louis Area (%) | Cape Girardeau and Sikeston Areas (%) |
|---|---|---|
| Fastened or secured objects in home | 13.0 | 32.0 |
| Stored canned food or water | 36.3 | 70.4 |
| Learned how to turn off utilities | 60.7 | 74.4 |
| Purchased earthquake insurance | 50.1 | 64.0 |
| | | |
| None of the above | 20.9 | 10.6 |
| 1 of the above | 28.9 | 11.2 |
| 2 of the above | 26.9 | 23.0 |
| 3 of the above | 15.6 | 33.5 |
| All 4 of the above | 7.8 | 21.7 |
| | $N = 398$ | $N = 161$ |

hood that the action will be taken (Mileti, Fitzpatrick, and Farhar, 1990: 94; 1992; Mileti and O'Brien, 1992). A large number of people take actions that are relatively easy to take, like storing food and water and knowing how to shut off utilities. Fewer will take actions that require more effort, such as making structural alterations or even fastening objects that might fall.

In the St. Louis area, about half of those surveyed had taken at least two of these four actions, and 23 percent had taken three or more. In the Cape Girardeau/Sikeston areas, more than 75 percent had taken at least two actions, and the majority had taken at least three of the four.

To what extent were these preparatory actions stimulated by the Browning prediction? The ideal way to answer this question would be to have measures of the number of people who had taken these protective actions before Browning made his prediction. That information was not available for the specific area we studied. However, Nigg (1987) did measure preparedness in the mid-1980s in a New Madrid regional sample that included St. Louis (as well as Memphis and seven other cities of various sizes). She found that 32 percent had stored food and 10 percent had stored water, and 13 percent had purchased earthquake insurance. She did not have comparable measures of our other two preparedness actions. Clearly, many more households had earthquake insurance at the time of our survey than at the time of Nigg's; in addition, a larger proportion of respondents in Cape Girardeau and Sikeston had stored food and water than had reported doing so at the time of her survey. Our figures for St. Louis were similar to hers for storage of food and water. These findings suggest an improvement in preparedness on both items in Cape Girardeau and Sikeston and on insurance in St. Louis. However, the comparability of the two studies is limited by the different wording of items and by the fact that the two studies asked about different preparedness actions.

Fortunately, it is also possible to assess the effect of the Browning prediction indirectly. This can be done by examining the correlation between believing the Browning prediction and taking these actions. We did this by comparing people who gave responses on the "likely" side of the scale to those who gave responses on the "unlikely" side of the scale on the question of the probability of a December earthquake. These data are shown in table 3-9. The table shows clearly that people who took Iben Browning's December 3 earthquake prediction seriously generally took more of these actions than did others. This difference holds for all forms of preparation except knowing how to turn utilities off—which a number of respondents volunteered that they already knew how to do before the earthquake forecast. Also, there is a very clear correlation between believing the Browning prediction and the number of actions taken. Those who thought that a December earthquake was at least somewhat likely were significantly more likely to have taken at least three of the four preparatory actions than those who thought it unlikely. On the basis of these findings, it appears virtually certain that the Browning prediction did stimulate preparedness: If people believed it, they were more likely to prepare.

While there was a clear correlation between believing the prediction and taking actions to prepare for an earthquake, the data on preparation reinforce the notion that the cognitive and behavioral dimensions of response to warnings are distinct. To an even larger extent than they were correlated with believing the prediction, preparatory actions were correlated with plans to make schedule changes around December 3. In this case, the relationship was statistically significant for all four types of preparations. And people who planned schedule changes were twice as likely as those who did not to have taken three or more preparatory actions. Again, this strongly supports the notion that the Browning prediction did stimulate people to prepare for an earthquake.

Table 3-9. Percentage of People Who Had Taken Steps to Prepare for an Earthquake (October 1990) by Perceived Likelihood of a Quake and Planned Schedule Changes

| | Thought December Quake Very/Somewhat Likely (%) | Thought December Quake Not Too Likely/ Very Unlikely (%) | Planned Changes (%) | Did Not Plan Changes (%) |
|---|---|---|---|---|
| Fastened or secured objects in home | 23.3 | 9.6 | 33.2 | 11.8 |
| | $N = 478$  Chi$^2$ = 13.34 df = 1  p < .0003 | | $N = 557$  Chi$^2$ = 35.35 df = 1  p < .0001 | |
| Stored canned food or water | 54.4 | 37.3 | 66.1 | 37.2 |
| | $N = 475$  Chi$^2$ = 12.29 df = 1  p < .0005 | | $N = 554$  Chi$^2$ = 40.03 df = 1  p < .0001 | |
| Learned how to turn off utilities | 65.1 | 67.8 | 74.7 | 62.7 |
| | $N$=472  Chi$^2$ = 0.89 df = 1  n.s. | | $N = 548$  Chi$^2$ = 11.33 df = 1  p < .004 | |
| Purchased earthquake insurance | 61.2 | 50.3 | 67.6 | 49.7 |
| | $N = 469$  Chi$^2$ = 4.92 df = 1  p < .03 | | $N = 535$  Chi$^2$ = 14.94 df = 1  p < .0001 | |
| Did at least 3 of the above | 38.5 | 24.6 | 50.0 | 25.1 |
| | $N = 462$  Chi$^2$ = 8.78 df = 1  p < .003 | | $N = 535$  Chi$^2$ = 32.23 df = 1  p < .0001 | |

## Preparedness Findings from Other New Madrid Surveys

Our survey was just one of a number of surveys on earthquake preparedness conducted by social researchers in the New Madrid Seismic Zone in the fall of 1990. Many of these researchers reported their findings at the research conference held at Southern Illinois University at Edwardsville in May 1991 and in the November 1993 special issue of the *International Journal of Mass Emergencies and Disasters*. In this section, we shall address the findings of these studies regarding various aspects of earthquake preparedness in the fall of 1990. We shall discuss insurance separately from other aspects of preparedness, because a particularly large number of the studies addressed that issue.

**Earthquake Insurance.** The studies are remarkably consistent with one another and with our findings with respect to earthquake insurance. Every study conducted during the October–November period found that 50 percent or more of the respondents in earthquake-prone areas reported having earthquake insurance. This pattern held for Memphis (Edwards, 1991, 1993), the St. Louis area (Farley et al., 1991a; Sylvester, 1991), Cape Girardeau and Sikeston, Missouri (Farley et al., 1991a), southern Indiana (Kennedy, 1991), and small Missouri and Arkansas towns immediately adjacent to the New Madrid fault zone (Showalter, 1991a, 1991b, 1993a). The average response was around 55 percent. These percentages are higher than those in California, which has led some researchers to question their validity. It was suggested, for example, that some people do not really know whether they have earthquake coverage. Yet the consistency of the figures is remarkable, and researchers (e.g., Kennedy, 1991) who spoke with insurance company representatives were told that sales of earthquake insurance were extensive.

In fact, the self-report data in these surveys are quite consistent with insurance company data on policies sold. A survey of twenty-five insurers serving the seven states of the New Madrid Seismic Zone found that the proportion of homeowners who had purchased earthquake insurance rose from 12 percent in 1989 to 37 percent in December 1990—a higher percentage than in California. In Kentucky, 60 percent had done so, and in Missouri, nearly 50 percent (Chartered Property and Casualty Underwriters, 1992). These figures undoubtedly understate insurance rates in the actual New Madrid Seismic

Zone, since some heavily populated parts of these states are in areas of low seismic risk. Western Missouri, for example, which includes the Kansas City metropolitan area, is a low-risk area in which relatively few people would be likely to purchase earthquake insurance. Undoubtedly, the actual number of those with earthquake insurance is well below the 50 percent statewide figure there, but well above it in the at-risk St. Louis area. One possible explanation for why earthquake insurance may be more widely purchased in the Midwest and mid-South than in California is that it is far more expensive in California than in the New Madrid Seismic Zone.

It also appears that sales of earthquake insurance continued at least up to December 3, and that, following the predicted date of the earthquake, a higher percentage of people had insurance than at the time of most of the surveys discussed above. Farley et al. (1991b) and Kennedy (1991) asked about insurance in follow-up surveys in February and April respectively, and found that 73 percent of respondents in southern Indiana and 71 percent of respondents in a combined St. Louis area/Cape Girardeau/Sikeston sample had earthquake insurance by then. Also suggestive of the same trend is comparison of our October survey in the St. Louis area with the November survey by Sylvester (1991). While the October survey found that 50.1 percent of St. Louis area respondents had purchased earthquake insurance, that percentage rose to 64 percent in the November survey. Data from the State Farm Insurance Company show that about 650,000 customers in the New Madrid region bought earthquake insurance in 1990, mainly in October and November (Johnson et al., cited in Kunreuther, 1993). By December 1991, a year after the predicted earthquake had failed to materialize, a survey of insurance companies showed that the proportion of homeowners in the seven-state area with earthquake insurance had fallen only slightly. At that time, 35 percent of homeowners had earthquake insurance—still more than in California (Chartered Property and Casualty Underwriters, 1992; Kunreuther, 1993). And once again, this figure includes data from parts of the seven states, such as areas like Kansas City, that have relatively low seismic risk. From all these data, it is clear that the Browning prediction led large numbers of people to add earthquake insurance to their homeowners' policies. In fact, people in the New Madrid region are better insured than people in other regions of the country at similar or greater seismic risk.

**Preparation and Mitigation.** The results of the various surveys, summarized in table 3-10, show that most people think preparation is a good idea, and that a sizable proportion have taken at least some steps to prepare for an earthquake. In fact, most surveys that measured various actions that might be taken found that a large proportion of people took more than one action. In general, the highest proportion of people took the easiest measures, such as having a working flashlight, having a battery-operated radio, and knowing how to shut off their utilities. Clearly, many of these are actions that people would take anyway, even in the absence of a specific earthquake threat. However, at least one survey (ours) indicated that those who believed the forecast were most likely to have taken such actions, and it also appears that the number of people who took such actions increased as the forecast date approached. Many had also stored food and water or other supplies—a number of surveys asked about this, and they found that 30–50 percent had done so; in some cases, the percentage was higher. On the other hand, most of the surveys, including ours, showed that more difficult actions, such as structural alterations of homes and securing of water heaters and other hazardous objects, had been taken by far fewer people. Nonetheless, the results as a whole suggest that (1) a norm in support of earthquake preparedness and mitigation arose in the New Madrid Seismic Zone following Browning's prediction, (2) many people took one or more actions to prepare for an earthquake, even if they were generally the easier actions to take, and (3) the Browning prediction, along with other events such as the Loma Prieta earthquake, does appear to have contributed to increased earthquake preparedness in the Midwest and mid-South.

*Findings from the February Survey*

It is apparent from the February survey data that the preparations we measured in October continued after our October survey was taken. The responses to the questions about preparation from both the October and February surveys are shown in table 3-11 for a combined sample of St. Louis area, Cape Girardeau, and Sikeston respondents. As with other items involving comparisons of the October and February surveys, we show the October data for the full sample, constant households, and constant individuals. The February data are shown for constant households (which constitute the entire February sample) and for constant individuals.

Table 3-10. Findings of Other Surveys on Actions Taken to Prepare for a Damaging Earthquake (Fall 1990)

| Atwood, 1993 | "Have you done anything to make your home safer if there were an earthquake?" Yes 48% | |
|---|---|---|
| | | (%) |
| Edwards, 1991, 1993 | Store food/water | 37 |
| | Learn first aid | 45 |
| | Devise family plan | 37 |
| | Have working flashlight | 84 |
| | Have battery radio | 70 |
| | Protect glass or dishes | 11 |
| | Secure water heater | 9 |
| | Give children instructions | 44 |
| | Secure furniture | 3 |
| | Have an engineer assess home | 4 |
| | Make structural changes | 4 |
| Levenbach and England, 1991 | Mean number of six recommended precautions taken by respondents: 2.7. (This paper reported only the mean, not frequency distributions.) | |
| Major, 1991, 1993 | Collected data on preparedness in November and February surveys, but frequency distributions are not reported in this paper. | |
| | | (%) |
| Showalter, 1991b, 1993a | Attended earthquake meetings | 28 |
| | Prepared earthquake survival kit | 50 |
| | Made physical changes to home to reduce damage | 20 |
| | Did nothing and planned to do nothing | 16 |

Table 3-10 continued

Wetzel et al., 1991

From survey before December 3:
"There are a number of things people can do to
reduce their risk in a quake."

|  | (%) |
|---|---|
| Strongly agree | 24 |
| Agree | 41 |
| Slightly agree | 21 |
| Slightly disagree | 4 |
| Disagree | 5 |
| Strongly disagree | 4 |

Stockpiling food, preparing the home, buying
insurance, or making first aid kits for the
predicted quake is

|  | (%) |
|---|---|
| Extremely smart, serving a good purpose | 24 |
| Very smart | 31 |
| Somewhat smart | 31 |
| Neutral, neither | 11 |
| Somewhat dumb | 2 |
| Very dumb | 1 |
| Extremely dumb, a waste of time/money | 1 |

From survey 1–3 days after predicted quake date:

|  | (%) |
|---|---|
| Bought/made first aid kit | 16 |
| Read safety pamphlet | 44 |
| Stockpiled supplies (water, food) | 31 |
| Made escape routes from buildings | 19 |
| Prepared home, made modifications | 11 |

Table 3-11. Preparedness Indicators (October 1990 and Feburary 1991)

| | October 1990 | | | February 1991 | |
|---|---|---|---|---|---|
| | Full Sample (%) | Constant Households (%) | Constant Individuals (%) | Constant Households (%) | Constant Individuals (%) |
| **Secured objects?** | | | | | |
| Yes | 18.5 | 17.1 | 18.7 | 27.6 | 25.1 |
| No | 81.3 | 82.9 | 81.3 | 71.7 | 74.4 |
| Don't know | 0.2 | 0.0 | 0.0 | 0.7 | 0.5 |
| N | | 293 | 203 | 293 | 203 |
| **Stored food/water?** | | | | | |
| Yes | 46.2 | 51.2 | 51.2 | 70.5 | 71.8 |
| No | 53.4 | 48.1 | 48.8 | 29.5 | 28.2 |
| Don't know | 0.3 | 0.0 | 0.0 | 0.0 | 0.0 |
| N | | 291 | 201 | 292 | 202 |
| **Shut off utilities?** | | | | | |
| Yes | 64.7 | 65.9 | 68.2 | 87.3 | 86.6 |
| No | 34.8 | 31.4 | 31.8 | 12.0 | 13.4 |
| Don't know | 0.2 | 0.3 | 0.0 | 0.7 | 0.0 |
| N | | 286 | 198 | 292 | 202 |
| **Quake insurance?** | | | | | |
| Yes | 54.1 | 55.6 | 55.8 | 71.0 | 72.4 |
| No | 44.9 | 41.6 | 43.2 | 28.0 | 26.6 |
| Don't know | 1.0 | 0.7 | 1.0 | 1.0 | 1.0 |
| N | | 287 | 199 | 293 | 203 |

As noted above, we asked respondents in February 1991 about the same four preparedness indicators that we had asked about the previous October: securing objects that could fall during a quake, storing food and water, knowing how to shut off utilities, and having earthquake insurance. As shown in table 3-11, the proportion who had done all four of these things was higher in February than it had been in October. This was true for the whole February sample, and it was also true for those individuals who had also answered the October survey. It suggests very strongly that the increase in preparedness we noted in October continued between then and the predicted date of the earthquake. Moreover, it is encouraging that this high level of preparedness was sustained more than two months after the Browning forecast had been disconfirmed.

Has such preparedness continued over the longer term? Much as in Kennedy's findings (1991) from his surveys about earthquake risk in Indiana (although he used somewhat different measures), the increase in preparedness we observed between October and February contrasts with a decline in the percentage who think a major quake is likely in the next ten to fifteen years. The latter could, of course, portend a decline in preparedness, as the public turns its attention away from earthquake risk. In this context, it is important to note that most or all of the increase in preparedness between the October and February surveys probably occurred before December 3 (though our data offer no way to prove this). It is at least possible that people were more prepared on December 3 than they were when we took our February survey. On the other hand, some preparedness steps, such as fastening objects like water heaters and cabinets, learning how to turn off utilities, and possibly buying insurance, are unlikely to be reversed, at least so long as people remain at their present places of residence. Thus, there are reasons both to hope that preparedness has been sustained and to fear that it may not have.

Fortunately, we do not have to speculate, because we had the opportunity to conduct two more surveys, in July 1992 and May 1993. In the remainder of the book, we shall examine the longer-term trends and patterns displayed by those two surveys.

## Summary and Conclusions

In this chapter, we have seen that while many people planned changes in their schedules around December 3, significantly fewer actually did change their schedules. This appears virtually certain, even though dissonance reduction may have led to some understatement of the degree to which schedules were changed once the predicted earthquake had failed to materialize. Moreover, many of the schedule changes that did occur were the result of school cancellations or, less often, work closures. The effects of school cancellations are also a major reason why people with children were more likely to stay home from work on December 3 than people without children. These effects, combined with gender role differentiation, also help to explain why women were more likely than men to change their work schedules. Although most schedule changes were prompted by school closings, it is nonetheless true that at least some people kept their children home from school even when school was not canceled. Moreover, people who believed Browning's prediction were more likely to keep their children home from school than people who did not, as were people who had told us in the October survey that they planned to change their schedules around December 3. People who said in October that they thought a December earthquake was likely also retrospectively reported higher levels of concern about the prediction when we conducted the follow-up survey in February 1991.

The February survey also revealed that there were improvements in earthquake preparedness that continued after early December, and that people continued to perceive their areas as being at risk for a damaging earthquake. The question of whether improvements in earthquake preparedness resulting from Browning's prediction continued in the years following 1991 is the subject to which we turn next, in chapter 4. In that chapter, we will also examine trends across our four surveys between 1990 and 1993 in awareness of and concern about the longer-term earthquake threat in the central United States.

# 4

# Trends in Awareness, Concern, and Preparedness, 1990–1993

AFTER COMPLETING THE October 1990 and February 1991 surveys, we received funding from the National Science Foundation to conduct two additional surveys. These surveys were conducted in July 1992 and May 1993, and again data were collected for the St. Louis metropolitan area, Cape Girardeau, and Sikeston. The surveys included expanded measurements of earthquake awareness, concern, and preparedness. However, certain items were retained across all four surveys in order to establish time trends for comparable items. Before discussing the methods and results of the 1992 and 1993 surveys, we shall briefly review the findings of past research on the longer-term effects of earthquake predictions on earthquake awareness and preparedness.

## Past Research on Longer-Term Effects of Earthquake Predictions

While the focus of our discussion thus far has been on the short-term effects of earthquake predictions, there have been a limited number of studies that have examined longer-term trends in earthquake awareness and preparedness following earthquake predictions. A potential problem in interpreting such research is that some earthquake predictions have been scientific in nature, others have been pseudoscientific, and, in at least a few cases, both types of predictions have been made in the same area at around the same time. A related problem is that in some instances, predictions (often, although not always, pseudoscientific ones) have focused on narrowly defined time periods such as a given day or a period of a week or two, while in other instances they have been much more diffuse, indicating a stated probability of an earthquake sometime over a period of several years. If an earthquake forecast is relatively nonspecific with respect to time or place and refers only to an increased probability (or to a wide range of probabilities), it is often called a "near-prediction." If the forecast is specific with respect to time, place, probability, and magnitude, it is a "true prediction" (Turner, Nigg, and Paz, 1986; Mileti, Fitzpatrick, and Farhar, 1990). If the forecast is also short-term, it may be considered a warning. For such a short-term prediction or warning to be useful, it must present some plausible evidence that the probability during a specified time period (months, days, or hours) exceeds the generally accepted base earthquake probability for that seismic area (Ad Hoc Working Group, 1990: 3). Obviously, the concepts of "near-prediction," "true prediction," and "warning" represent something of a continuum, and it is not always obvious how to classify a given forecast or statement. Often, both true predictions and near-predictions may be made for an earthquake-prone area over a relatively short time.

*Los Angeles in the Mid-1970s*

The research of Turner, Nigg, and Paz (1986), for example, examined a time period during the 1970s in which there were both scientific and pseudo-scientific statements indicating that portions of southern California might be about to experience an earthquake. The scientific statements in this instance took the form of near-predictions, whereas the pseudoscientific forecast took the form of a warning concerning a specific date. The initial scientific statement noted a possibly increased risk of an earthquake's arising from what became known as the "Palmdale bulge" or the "Southern California Uplift" — an area along the San Andreas Fault in which there had been a gradual and modest uplifting of the earth's surface. The most explicit statements concerning increased risk were issued in April 1976 by the California Seismic Safety Commission and by James Whitcomb, a Caltech seismologist. Whitcomb, in a statement he later retracted, stated that there was an increased likelihood of a quake of magnitude 5.5 to 6.5 over a one-year period in 1976 and 1977.

In November of the same year, a pseudoscientific forecast of a Los Angeles earthquake, to occur on December 20, 1976, was issued by Henry Minturn. Because it focused on a specific day, Minturn's pseudoscientific forecast can be classified as a true prediction or warning. As was noted in earlier chapters, Minturn, like Browning, made undocumented claims of past success at predicting earthquakes, lacked formal training in geology or seismology, and based his prediction on lunar gravitational forces. As with Browning, his claims of past successful predictions were at first accepted uncritically and reported by the news media. The predicted earthquake did not occur, and around the time that Minturn's forecast was disconfirmed, Whitcomb retracted his statement.

This series of events led to a great heightening of interest in earthquakes in the Los Angeles area, to numerous rumors, and to increased support for ongoing earthquake preparedness. However, this heightened interest did not for the most part translate into increased personal preparedness (Turner, Nigg, and Paz, 1986). It should be noted, however, that the surveys taken by Turner, Nigg, and Paz were conducted after the period covered by the Whitcomb statement and the Minturn warning, and thus they could not establish a clear baseline of preparedness prior to those events. Turner, Nigg, and Paz continued to conduct surveys in the Los Angeles area from March 1977 through January 1979. They found that, following the initial surge of concern about earthquakes spawned by the Whitcomb statement and the Minturn forecast, preparedness remained fairly stable over a period of more than two years. This suggests that the level of preparedness may not fall following a period of heightened concern. If this pattern were to hold in the New Madrid Seismic Zone, preparedness gains resulting from the Browning event might be sustained for at least a few years following the prediction. However, the NMSZ differs from Los Angeles in that earthquake awareness was lower prior to the Browning event, earthquakes occur less frequently than in Los Angeles, and thus the entire earthquake issue had less salience in the NMSZ than in Los Angeles prior to the period of heightened awareness.

Another key finding of the Turner, Nigg, and Paz study, which was supported by our own research in the NMSZ (Farley et al., 1991b, 1991c), was that responses to the forecasts were not much influenced by whether the forecast came from a scientific or pseudoscientific source. Rather, people considered both scientific and pseudoscientific sources of information, used what they saw as useful from each, and did not always distinguish between the two (Turner, Nigg, and Paz, 1986).

One key similarity between the Los Angeles area and the NMSZ is that, in both cases, there were both a pseudoscientific "true prediction" or warning as well as more scientific near-predictions. Also, in both cases there was heightened interest in earthquakes, in Los Angeles because of the Palmdale bulge and the Minturn forecast, and in the NMSZ because of the 1989 Loma Prieta earthquake and the Browning forecast. In the NMSZ, these events led to greater attention to scientific near-predictions (contained in earlier statements by seismologists) that had placed the chance of a magnitude 6.0 quake in the New Madrid fault zone between the years 1990 and 2000 at between 13 and 63 percent.

### The Parkfield Earthquake Prediction Experiment

Another study of response to an earthquake prediction was conducted by Mileti, Fitzpatrick, and Farhar (1990, 1992; Mileti and Fitzpatrick, 1993). This study examined public response to the Parkfield Earthquake Prediction Experiment, a long-term earthquake forecast issued by the U.S. Geological Survey on April 5, 1985. The forecast predicted a 90 percent chance of a Richter magnitude 5.5–6.0 earthquake centered near Parkfield, California, sometime during the period between 1985 and 1993, with the possibility of a quake as strong as 7.0. This forecast might be regarded as a near-prediction, as it covers a wide time range. However, it is quite specific with respect to magnitude and geography, and it specifies a very high probability of a strong quake. In those regards it might be viewed as a true prediction, though clearly not a warning, because it is long-term in nature. In fact, it included statements to the effect that, if warranted at some time in the future, warnings for seventy-two-hour periods would be issued, although there was no guarantee that a major Parkfield earthquake would be preceded by such warnings.

In the spring of 1988, the state of California mailed a brochure about the prediction and earthquake preparedness to all households in the affected area. While the Mileti, Fitzpatrick, and Farhar study was not longitudinal, their survey research was conducted in 1989, four years after the prediction was initially issued, and about a year after the brochure was mailed. That should be a sufficiently long time to make some judgment as to whether the prediction had lasting effects on preparedness, or whether it merely provoked one or two brief flurries of concern that were forgotten as time passed. The circumstances differ from those of the Browning prediction in that (1) the prediction is scientific; (2) it covers an extended time, not a period of a few days (it is a long-term prediction or a near-prediction, rather than a warning); and (3) portions of the area for which it was issued (i.e., the Coalinga, California, area) had had recent experience with a damaging earthquake. However, there were also similarities to the NMSZ in that the issuance of the prediction was accompanied by considerable public and media attention, which subsequently fell off, and there was a probabilistic statement that an earthquake might occur at any time over an extended period, as was being stated in the NMSZ by seismological researchers. In other words, quite apart from the Browning prediction, the NMSZ was also (and still is) covered by a near-prediction, though it was not described as a "prediction experiment" as in the Parkfield case. While the NMSZ probabilities are more varied and not as high as those in the Parkfield area, both areas are similar in that they experienced a burst of attention to earthquakes followed by a prolonged period in which the area was identified by seismologists as having a significant risk of an earthquake on the order of magnitude 6.0, with a lesser chance of a stronger quake.

Mileti, Fitzpatrick, and Farhar (1990, 1992) studied three communities in the region covered by the Parkfield prediction. One of them, Coalinga, had experienced a damaging earthquake in 1983; the other two, Paso Robles and Taft, had had no recent experience of damaging earthquakes. The survey revealed that a large majority of people had heard about the Parkfield prediction: more than 93 percent in Coalinga, 88 percent in Paso Robles, and 65 percent in Taft. Nonetheless, the latter, in particular, is somewhat lower than the proportion in the NMSZ who had heard about the Browning forecast, which was consistently shown by surveys to have been in the 95–100 percent range. Thus, in the Parkfield situation, unlike that in New Madrid, it appears there was a significant minority who had not heard the prediction and therefore could not be expected to react to it. It should be noted, however, that the lower percentages in Parkfield may also have arisen from the fact that it had been a year since the questionnaires were mailed and four years since the forecast was first issued; the NMSZ surveys were conducted while the Browning forecast was still current news. With respect to the Parkfield prediction, it should be noted that people tended to remember that there had been a prediction of an earthquake sometime in the next few years, but they knew much less about the specifics of the prediction, such as the likely magnitude of the quake, the level of damage it would cause, the probability that it would occur, or the time frame covered by the forecast (Mileti, Fitzpatrick, and Farhar, 1990: 78–79).

The survey did, however, reveal that a large proportion of the population in the three areas—43–53 percent—believed that they or their families would be affected by a Parkfield earthquake "in the next few years." While there was no preforecast survey with which to compare these results, they nonetheless represent a much higher proportion expecting to be personally affected than is typically found in surveys concerning earthquake risk (Mileti, Fitzpatrick, and Farhar, 1990; Mileti et al., 1981). Thus it appears that the prediction led to a heightened sense of personal risk and that this sense was sustained four years after the forecast was initially issued and one year after the brochure was mailed out.

While there was a heightened sense of personal risk, only sometimes did that translate into taking actions for mitigation or to improve preparedness. Sizable minorities reported having learned what to do in preparation for an earthquake: stockpiling emergency supplies, purchasing earthquake insurance, and securing certain items to make them safer in case of a quake. None of those actions, even the relatively easy ones, had been taken by as many as one-third of the respondents reported on by Mileti, Fitzpatrick, and Farhar (1990). Nonetheless, the authors concluded (p. 102) that the level of preparedness was higher at the time of their survey than it would have been had the prediction not been issued: "Consequently, many Coalinga, Paso Robles, and Taft citizens are better equipped to face the next Parkfield earthquake as a direct result of informing the public about the earthquake prediction."

The study also found that people with previous experience with damaging earthquakes, people who had taken preparation or mitigation actions prior to the issuance of the Parkfield prediction, and people whose friends and neighbors were taking actions to prepare for the earthquake were the most likely to have taken preparation or mitigation actions. The latter finding is consistent with findings regarding plans to take action in response to Browning's forecast in the NMSZ (Farley et al., 1991a). In general, the Mileti, Fitzpatrick, and Farhar (1990) study revealed that the most likely to respond to the prediction were those who perceived that the information they had received about the Parkfield earthquake prediction was consistent, from multiple sources and communication channels, and specific with respect to magnitude and damage potential and what should be done. Because of Coalinga's recent experience with a damaging earthquake, the response there was stronger than in the other communities.

## The Tokai, Japan, Earthquake Prediction

In Japan, a long-term forecast was issued in 1976 for the Tokai region, including the Shizouka area, where the potential for casualties is greatest (Hirose, 1986). The forecast received substantial news media coverage when issued, then lower levels of media attention from 1977 through 1983. Hirose conducted a four-wave panel study in the cities of Atami and Ito in the Shizouka Prefecture. The surveys were conducted in August 1980, February 1981, October 1981, and January 1983. Retrospective questions in the 1980 survey indicated that most respondents were more concerned about the possibility of an earthquake than they had been a year earlier; after that time, respondents described their level of concern as remaining the same. Questions on how worried people were about earthquakes, how dangerous they thought their area was in terms of earthquakes, and the effectiveness of preparation produced relatively constant responses throughout the study period.

Hirose interpreted the findings from this study as showing that the residents were aware of the earthquake risk and that the Tokai Earthquake Prediction and related news media coverage had heightened that awareness—but that at the same time, awareness had reached a plateau and was not rising further. Although awareness was no longer rising, it also did not fall off appreciably, even several years after the issuance of the forecast and the accompanying flurry of media attention. However, while awareness was high, the study also found a good deal of fatalism: Around 50 to 55 percent in each of the four surveys felt that "mass-scale casualties will occur regardless," as opposed to "Casualties can be kept to a minimum." These results suggest that increases in awareness of earthquake risk can be sustained for extended periods following announcements of forecasts and the resultant burst of media attention. In another paper, Hirose and Ishizuka (1983) reported some increase of preparedness over the first three waves of the study, again suggesting a sustained effect. The Tokai situation differs from the New Madrid situation in that there was no warning, pseudoscientific or otherwise—merely a probabilistic near-prediction or long-term prediction.

## Earthquake Predictions in China

The greatest successes in the short-term prediction of earthquakes have occurred in China. On several occasions, the Chinese government has issued short-term earthquake warnings, and in some of those cases damaging earthquakes have occurred. The most clear, unqualified success was the Haicheng earthquake on February 4, 1975, a magnitude 7.4 quake for which a warning was issued several hours before it occurred (Turner, Nigg, and Paz, 1986: 4; Mileti and Fitzpatrick, 1993: 49). Mileti, Fitzpatrick, and Farhar (1990: 2) note two other instances of successful short-term earthquake predictions in China: near the Burmese border in 1976 and at Sungpan-Pingwu in Szechuan Province later that year. Property loss and human injury were minimized by actions taken in response to at least two of these warnings.

Unfortunately, while the Chinese have been able on a few occasions to predict earthquakes, they have not been able to do so consistently. In some instances, strong earthquakes are preceded by foreshocks or earthquake clusters, but in many others they are not. Hence there have been both false predictions of damaging earthquakes and damaging earthquakes that have occurred with no warning. There was, for example, no such short-term warning of China's most devastating earthquake, the Tangshan quake of July 1976, which is estimated to have taken nearly a quarter million lives (Li, 1991; Mileti and Fitzpatrick, 1993: 49). There had, however, been a near-prediction, or what the Chinese government calls a medium-term prediction. The Tangshan area had been included in a rather large area of northeastern China including Beijing in which it was stated that a quake of Richter magnitude 5.0–6.0 was possible at some time in a 1–2 year period. This near-prediction had been issued slightly over two years before the Tangshan quake occurred (Li, 1991). Early in 1976, the State Seismological Bureau held a meeting in Beijing in which it was determined that seismic risk remained high in northeastern China and that a quake of up to magnitude 7.0 could occur somewhere in that region.

In China, only short-term warnings (in which an earthquake is expected within a span of fifteen days or less) are issued to the public. Medium-term predictions are issued only to local governments, the army, and other governmental agencies involved in emergency preparedness and response. Hence, there was no public statement about the risk of an earthquake in the Tangshan area; rather, it was part of a large area in which officials had been alerted to an ongoing risk of a damaging earthquake and in which they were engaging in both seismic monitoring and preparedness activities (Li, 1991). The latter included presentations to the public about earthquake risk and preparedness and distribution of pamphlets on these subjects. Unfortunately, the monitoring did not detect any anomalies prior to the devastating quake.

Studies following the Tangshan earthquake suggest that there was some public awareness of the near-prediction prior to the 1976 earthquake. Qijia, Tuo, and Zhizhou (1990), for example, point out that the earthquake preparedness activities of local governments enabled some people to become aware that the area was thought to be at risk, and that those people then communicated that information to their relatives and friends. While retrospective surveys have problems of both recall and population turnover, results of a 1987 retrospective survey by Li (1991) are nonetheless instructive. Li reports that about half of the Tangshan respondents had heard that an earthquake might occur there, and that most had heard from either work units or friends and relatives—the sources one would expect, based on the Qijia, Tuo, and Zhizhou model of the means by which the forecast was disseminated. Of those who reported having heard the forecast before the earthquake occurred, more than one-third reported having been very concerned and another one-third said they had been somewhat concerned.

On one level, these results suggest that the medium-term prediction of a northeast China earthquake may have led to some sustained heightening of earthquake awareness, since it was issued more than two years before the earthquake occurred. However, it is difficult in a retrospective survey to tell just what time period people may have been referring to when they said they had been concerned, and the fact that such a devastating quake subsequently occurred may have led people, in retrospect, to say that they had been concerned even if they had not.

*Other Earthquake Predictions*

In at least two other instances, Wilmington, North Carolina, in 1976 and Lima, Peru, in 1981, predictions of earthquakes within a narrowly specified time and geographic location have attracted substantial mass media attention and elicited a substantial public response (Kerr, 1991; Olson, 1989; Echevarria, Norton, and Norton, 1986). In each of these cases, significant numbers of people appear to have taken preparatory actions and/or altered their schedules. These events were less thoroughly studied than some others, and time-series surveys were not conducted following the failure of the predictions. However, some evidence does exist regarding their short-term effects on earthquake awareness and preparedness.

The Wilmington prediction was made by a psychic, and, ironically, given enhanced credibility when it was backed by David Stewart, who was then an assistant professor of geology at the University of North Carolina at Chapel Hill. The psychic predicted a magnitude 8.0 earthquake in the Wilmington area during the third week of January 1976. According to Mileti and Fitzpatrick (1993: 52), research indicated that about 40 percent of the population took some kind of preparatory action and 17 percent stockpiled emergency supplies. About 30 percent of the population made efforts to obtain information about the earthquake prediction. On the other hand, about a third of the population "did not take the prediction seriously." The prediction did result in the sale of about six thousand earthquake insurance policies in the area, and retail business was reported to be slow on the day of the predicted earthquake, as was the case in the Browning episode.

In the Lima, Peru, incident, two American earthquake scientists predicted that an earthquake was likely to occur in the Lima area during the summer of 1981. This prediction had extensive political consequences, as reported by Olson (1989). It also appears to have stimulated preparedness: Echevarria, Norton, and Norton (1986) reported that over half of the population of Lima took some action to prepare. However, as in the case of the Wilmington prediction, we do not know to what extent these preparedness actions were sustained over the longer term.

## New Madrid in the 1990s: A Unique Research Opportunity

Taken together, the studies we have reviewed are suggestive of a pattern in which earthquake awareness rises with a forecast or other earthquake-related event that draws media attention, then levels off at a new, higher plateau. The evidence is less clear with respect to actual preparedness, although the Turner, Nigg, and Paz findings are suggestive of such a pattern in Los Angeles. However, prior to our series of surveys there was no set of time series data that assessed the longer-term effects of a disconfirmed earthquake warning (either pseudoscientific or scientific) on awareness and preparedness and that also contained awareness and preparedness measures (1) for times both before and for an extended period after the prediction was disconfirmed, and (2) in an area for which a long-term prediction or near-prediction was in effect—that is, an area which is identified as having a significant probability of a damaging earthquake over a period of several years. The Turner, Nigg, and Paz study contains every element except one: It lacks data prior to the date on which Minturn's forecast was disconfirmed and the time at which Whitcomb withdrew his statement about an increased risk arising from the Palmdale Bulge. Thus, all data from that study were taken from times that, to some extent, came after disconfirmed earthquake predictions.

Some of the studies that have been reported on the Browning forecast to date do contain measures before and after the disconfirmation of the forecast (e.g., Farley et al., 1991a, 1991b; Wetzel et al., 1991; Kennedy, 1991). However, these studies lack longer-term measures, because insufficient time had passed after the disconfirmation of the forecast. The other studies we have reviewed do present measures of earthquake awareness or preparedness for periods of up to several years after the issuance of long-term predictions or near-predictions, but they do not contain the element of a disconfirmed warning. Thus, the research being reported here addresses a situation that has not previously been researched.

Finally, it should be stressed that in addition to this, the regions in which other studies have been performed are different in important ways from the NMSZ. Southern California is clearly an area in which earthquake risk is well known and in which much of the population is experienced with earthquakes. Earthquakes (particularly strong ones) are considerably less frequent in the NMSZ, with the result that people are less experienced with them and, prior to the Loma Prieta quake and the Browning forecast, were less aware that they lived in an area of seismic risk. Experience has been shown by a number of studies to be an important factor in the response to earthquake forecasts. Mileti, Fitzpatrick, and Farhar (1990) found that those with earthquake experience were more likely to respond to the Parkfield Earthquake Prediction Experiment. In a somewhat similar vein, the study by Mulilis and Duval (1991) of UCLA students found sustained increases in preparedness following two damaging California earthquakes but only temporary increases following two minor quakes. Though tentative, this pattern of findings suggests that those with experience of damaging earthquakes may be more receptive to the idea of earthquake preparation.

On the other hand, the lack of experience of most people in the NMSZ has been cited as a key factor in the spread of the Browning scare (Kerr, 1991). It may be that experience with earthquakes increases the salience of the risk but also reduces the influence of pseudoscientific forecasts. It is clear that the

Browning forecast in the NMSZ had a larger impact than the Minturn forecast in southern California, though there are many possible reasons for that besides differences in experience with earthquakes. Still, experience with earthquake forecasts seems to be important enough a factor to place limitations on the comparability of California and the NMSZ. Even greater limitations exist in comparability for the Japanese and Chinese studies, since those involve areas not only with experiences different from those of the NMSZ but also with different cultures and social systems.

## Five Working Hypotheses

Despite the limitations discussed above, there are certain hypotheses that can be tentatively proposed. Among them are the following:

A. Surveys from 1992 and 1993 may reveal a somewhat more realistic assessment of earthquake likelihood—that is, less tendency than during the Browning forecast period to overestimate the probability of a damaging earthquake. However, it is to be expected that a clear majority of respondents will reveal a continuing awareness that the NMSZ is at risk for a damaging quake.

B. The majority of respondents can still be expected to have earthquake insurance. It is possible, however, that the economic recession of the early 1990s may have led some not to renew their insurance as their policies came due in 1991–92, so that the percentage with earthquake insurance may have fallen somewhat below the levels reported in early 1991.

C. It is to be expected that levels of household preparedness would not be greater than they were just after the disconfirmation of the Browning forecast; it seems likely that a peak in preparedness was attained around the predicted date for the earthquake. However, household preparedness is still likely to be better than it was prior to the sequence of events beginning with Loma Prieta and culminating with the Browning prediction.

D. The types of preparedness actions most likely to be sustained will be the ones that are hardest to take and also hardest to reverse, such as fastening down objects and making structural alterations. On the other hand, stocks of food, water, and other supplies may be used up and not replaced.

E. Higher levels of preparedness are likely among those whose friends and neighbors are continuing to take preparedness actions, among those with a greater awareness of earthquake risk, among those with greater knowledge about what to do during an earthquake, and among those who perceive that they or their neighborhood are at greater risk of damage from an earthquake.

## Methodology for the 1992 and 1993 Surveys

The methodology of the 1992 and 1993 surveys was very similar to the methodology of the first survey, conducted in October 1990, with two important exceptions. As in the October survey, the later surveys used randomly selected residential telephone numbers in Cape Girardeau, Missouri; Sikeston, Missouri; and the St. Louis metropolitan area (defined for purposes of the surveys as St. Louis City, St. Louis County, Jefferson and St. Charles counties, Missouri, and Madison and St. Clair counties, Illinois). The first difference in methodology from the October survey is that we were able to obtain a sampling frame including unlisted numbers for Cape Girardeau and Sikeston. That enabled us to conduct a random sample of all households with telephones, as we had done for the St. Louis area in the October survey.

The surveys were conducted from July 19 to 27, 1992, and April 25 to May 3, 1993. The random-digit dialing procedure sampled from all possible numbers within the target areas, except that known business numbers were deleted. The working ranges of numbers and the known business numbers for the St. Louis metropolitan area are contained in a file used for telephone surveys by Regional Research and Development Services (RRDS) of Southern Illinois University at Edwardsville, which had also conducted the October 1990 and February 1991 surveys. In addition, RRDS purchased a similar file of telephone numbers from Survey Sampling, Inc., for Cape Girardeau and Sikeston. This was done because the RRDS file contains only numbers for the St. Louis metropolitan area. Because of the short time frame before the date of Browning's predicted earthquake, we had been unable to do this for the October survey. The longer planning time for the 1992 and 1993 surveys allowed us to use this more representative sampling methodology.

The second difference in methodology is that we sampled a fixed number of households in each area, then surveyed as many of those households as we

Table 4-1. Geographic Distribution of Actual Households, Households Called, and Surveys Completed (July 1992 and May 1993)

| | Percentage of Actual Households | Valid Households Called | | | | Surveys Completed | | | |
| | | July 1992 | | May 1993 | | July 1992 | | May 1993 | |
| | | Number | Percent | Number | Percent | Number | Percent | Number | Percent |
|---|---|---|---|---|---|---|---|---|---|
| Madison Co. | 10.73 | 162 | 10.47 | 156 | 9.99 | 77 | 12.92 | 88 | 13.08 |
| St. Clair Co. | 10.95 | 180 | 11.64 | 171 | 10.95 | 67 | 11.24 | 77 | 11.44 |
| St. Charles Co. | 8.36 | 125 | 8.08 | 126 | 8.07 | 42 | 7.05 | 57 | 8.47 |
| Jefferson Co. | 6.73 | 97 | 6.27 | 105 | 6.72 | 46 | 7.72 | 39 | 5.79 |
| St. Louis City | 20.64 | 311 | 20.10 | 301 | 19.27 | 93 | 15.60 | 112 | 16.64 |
| St. Louis Co. | 42.59 | 672 | 43.44 | 703 | 45.01 | 271 | 45.47 | 300 | 44.58 |
| Total MSA* | 100.00 | 1,547 | 100.00 | 1,562 | 100.00 | 596 | 100.00 | 673 | 100.00 |

*Metropolitan statistical area

could reach. This constitutes sampling without replacement of households we were unable to reach. In the earlier surveys, we had simply continued sampling and calling until the desired number of households was achieved. That methodology constituted sampling with replacement, because if a household did not answer we sampled another until the desired number was attained. The method used in the 1992 and 1993 surveys, sampling without replacement, is desirable in that it is a true "Equal Probability of Selection Method" (EPSEM) sample: Each household in each county has a known and equal chance of getting into the sample. That is not the case in sampling methods that use replacement. On the other hand, a risk using this method is that if response rates are unequal in different areas within the larger area where the sampling is done, the sample may be geographically unrepresentative.

### The Geography of the St. Louis Area Sample

In each county of the St. Louis metropolitan area, telephone numbers were sampled from the county in proportion to the county's share of the metropolitan area's population. This was done because the RRDS telephone number files were separate by county. In all of the geographic areas we surveyed, our phone number lists included some numbers that had been disconnected. In general, the disconnect rates were similar, except that in the St. Louis area, two counties, St. Clair and Jefferson, had abnormally high disconnect rates compared with the rest of the area. The number of calls attempted in those counties was adjusted upward during the 1992 survey from what had been originally planned in order to offset the high disconnect rates. That allowed us to attempt to contact a number of households in each county that was proportionate to that county's share of the metropolitan area's population. This procedure was repeated in the 1993 survey. In all other counties, the number of calls attempted was as originally planned in both surveys. As is shown in table 4-1, the proportion of calls to valid household telephone numbers in each county in the St. Louis metropolitan area closely corresponded in both surveys to the proportion of households in each county as of the 1990 census.

For the part of the survey covering the St. Louis area, we examined the distribution of counties among actual households, valid numbers called, and completed surveys. These distributions are also shown in table 4-1. From a strict methodological standpoint, the Percentage of Valid Households Called column is the one it is most important to match with the actual distribution of households, because that ensures that each household has an equal chance of being called. In general, as noted above, we were very much on target. These proportions correspond closely to the proportions of households in each county, indicated in column 1 of table 4-1. The right-hand columns indicate the distribution of actual responses. Though still generally proportionate, these vary somewhat more because of variations in the refusal rate. The one sizable deviation is that we underrepresented St. Louis City because of the high refusal rate there. The 1992 refusal rate in the city was 62.7 percent, the highest anywhere in the metro area. We somewhat overrepresented Madison County, and to a lesser extent St. Louis County, because the refusal rates were lower there than elsewhere in the metropolitan area. The lowest refusal rate was in Madison County, where it was 42.2 percent.

*Refusals*

The number of calls attempted and the number and proportion of (1) bad numbers/disconnects, (2) valid households, (3) households not reached because the line was busy or because there was no answer after six attempts, (4) valid households actually reached, (5) refusals, and (6) surveys completed are shown in table 4-2 for both surveys. In general, the refusal rate for the first survey, just over 50 percent, was quite high. This is a higher refusal rate than was observed in either of two previous earthquake surveys conducted by the principal investigator in the same three areas in October 1990 and February 1991. A number of factors may account for this high rate: less interest in the earthquake issue than at the time of Browning's prediction, increasing resistance caused by growing numbers of telephone surveys and solicitations, growing use of answering machines, and perhaps the fact that this survey was done in the summer and thus had to compete with outdoor activities, yard work, vacations, and so forth.

In the second survey, an adjustment in procedure was made to attempt to reduce the refusal rate. When a respondent refused to participate in the survey, interviewers were instructed to ask whether it would be more convenient if they called back at a later time. Some respondents said yes, and the response rate for the second survey was modestly higher than in the first. The proportion refusing the survey fell in all three areas in the second survey, ranging from just under 50 percent in the St. Louis area to a little below 44 percent in Sikeston. Although lower, this refusal rate is still relatively high, and the relatively high refusal rates in the two surveys underline the importance of examining the representativeness of the sample.

Table 4-2. Response Rates by Geographic Region

| | July 1992 | | | May 1993 | | |
|---|---|---|---|---|---|---|
| | St. Louis Metro | Cape Girardeau | Sikeston | St. Louis Metro | Cape Girardeau | Sikeston |
| Telephone numbers attempted | 2,328 | 591 | 592 | 2,359 | 599 | 600 |
| Bad numbers/disconnects | 811 | 123 | 121 | 797 | 138 | 146 |
| Percentage of total attempts | 34.8 | 17.4 | 20.4 | 33.8 | 23.0 | 24.3 |
| Valid households called | 1,517 | 468 | 471 | 1,562 | 461 | 454 |
| Percentage of total attempts | 65.2 | 79.2 | 79.6 | 66.2 | 77.0 | 75.7 |
| No answer/busy, 6 attempts | 209 | 36 | 51 | 220 | 50 | 51 |
| Valid households reached | 1,308 | 432 | 420 | 1,342 | 411 | 403 |
| Percentage of total attempts | 56.2 | 73.1 | 70.9 | 56.9 | 68.6 | 67.2 |
| Percentage of valid households | 86.2 | 92.3 | 89.2 | 85.9 | 89.2 | 88.8 |
| Refused | 716 | 221 | 198 | 669 | 184 | 176 |
| Percentage of valid households | 47.2 | 47.2 | 42.0 | 42.8 | 39.9 | 38.8 |
| Percentage of households reached | 54.7 | 51.2 | 47.1 | 49.9 | 44.8 | 43.7 |
| Completed survey | 592 | 211 | 222 | 673 | 227 | 227 |
| Percentage of valid households | 39.0 | 45.1 | 47.1 | 43.1 | 49.2 | 50.0 |
| Percentage of households reached | 45.3 | 48.8 | 52.9 | 50.1 | 55.2 | 56.3 |

## How Representative Were Our Samples?

The social characteristics of those who responded are shown in table 4-3, and they are presented in the table along with data on the target populations to assess representativeness with respect to sociodemographic characteristics. It should be noted that racial composition for the population is based on the racial composition of the 1990 population aged eighteen and over. This is done for comparability, as we spoke only to persons eighteen and over. Age and education are based on population data; presence of children, housing tenure, and income are based on household data.

Table 4-3. Selected Demographic Characteristics of Survey Samples and Survey Area Populations

| Characteristic | St. Louis Metro Area | | | Cape Girardeau | | | Sikeston | | |
|---|---|---|---|---|---|---|---|---|---|
| | 1992 Sample (%) | 1993 Sample (%) | 1990 Pop. (%) | 1992 Sample (%) | 1993 Sample (%) | 1990 Pop. (%) | 1992 Sample (%) | 1993 Sample (%) | 1990 Pop. (%) |
| Age | | | | | | | | | |
| 18–30 | 23.3 | 22.6 | 24.8 | 21.8 | 22.5 | 35.0 | 29.3 | 15.7 | 23.0 |
| 30–49 | 44.3 | 48.0 | 40.0 | 37.1 | 41.9 | 31.4 | 43.3 | 43.2 | 37.4 |
| 50–64 | 18.9 | 15.4 | 18.2 | 22.3 | 21.6 | 15.0 | 13.0 | 20.1 | 18.5 |
| 65 & over | 13.5 | 14.1 | 17.3 | 18.8 | 14.0 | 18.6 | 14.4 | 21.0 | 21.0 |
| Race | | | | | | | | | |
| White | 85.6 | 84.5 | 82.0 | 90.7 | 94.1 | 91.8 | 91.3 | 87.3 | 86.6 |
| Black | 12.3 | 12.6 | 16.5 | 7.9 | 3.2 | 6.5 | 5.3 | 11.4 | 12.7 |
| Other | 2.1 | 2.3 | 1.5 | 1.3 | 2.7 | 1.7 | 3.3 | 1.3 | 0.7 |
| Marital status | | | | | | | | | |
| Married | 57.8 | 59.7 | 54.5 | 66.0 | 64.0 | 48.5 | 55.5 | 58.8 | 56.1 |
| Divorced/separated | 12.9 | 12.3 | 11.1 | 12.2 | 8.6 | 9.8 | 12.4 | 12.7 | 12.9 |
| Widowed | 7.4 | 7.4 | 8.1 | 8.7 | 7.7 | 8.3 | 8.6 | 10.1 | 10.4 |
| Single | 21.9 | 20.5 | 26.4 | 13.0 | 19.8 | 33.3 | 23.4 | 18.4 | 20.6 |
| Have kids under 18 | | | | | | | | | |
| Yes | 37.8 | 42.5 | 33.5 | 48.2 | 42.3 | 28.4 | 41.7 | 38.6 | 36.7 |
| Housing tenure | | | | | | | | | |
| Own | 70.9 | 74.0 | 67.9 | 69.3 | 74.5 | 57.4 | 62.1 | 72.9 | 59.1 |
| Education | | | | | | | | | |
| Less than 4 years high school | 7.2 | 5.9 | 24.0 | 16.4 | 9.0 | 33.0 | 8.7 | 11.6 | 35.0 |
| 4 years high school or GED | 25.8 | 29.7 | 30.0 | 39.8 | 28.1 | 28.2 | 26.4 | 39.6 | 35.0 |
| Some college | 34.5 | 34.1 | 25.4 | 28.3 | 31.2 | 24.5 | 37.0 | 24.9 | 16.2 |
| 4 years college or more | 32.5 | 30.3 | 20.7 | 15.5 | 31.7 | 24.3 | 27.9 | 24.0 | 13.8 |

Household income*

Table 4-3 continued

| | | | | | | | | | |
|---|---|---|---|---|---|---|---|---|---|
| Less than $20,000 | 17.3 | 19.0 | 21.9 | 27.2 | 19.6 | 35.9 | 24.3 | 26.4 | 39.0 |
| $20,000–39,000 | 36.2 | 35.8 | 32.8 | 44.2 | 39.7 | 35.1 | 39.2 | 40.8 | 33.8 |
| $40,000–69,000 | 30.9 | 31.9 | 36.2 | 21.4 | 31.4 | 26.8 | 24.3 | 24.4 | 22.6 |
| $70,000–99,000 | 10.2 | 10.0 | 5.0 | 5.3 | 7.2 | 2.8 | 6.6 | 5.0 | 2.5 |
| $100,000 or more | 5.5 | 3.3 | 4.0 | 1.9 | 2.1 | 2.5 | 5.5 | 3.5 | 2.2 |
| Gender | | | | | | | | | |
| Female | 60.3 | 63.6 | 53.5 | 67.2 | 65.3 | 54.2 | 59.8 | 70.6 | 61.3 |
| Male | 39.7 | 36.4 | 46.5 | 32.8 | 34.7 | 45.8 | 40.2 | 29.4 | 38.7 |

*Income categories for 1990 census data are less than $15,000, $15,000–34,999, $35,000–74,999, $75,000–99,999, and $100,000 or more.

For most characteristics, the proportions of the respondents with a given characteristic are usually within about 4 percentage points of the proportion in the population with that characteristic in the St. Louis area samples, and within about 7 points in the other samples. Thus, they fall within the margin of error for a sample of this size. There are three important exceptions. One involves an array of variables in Cape Girardeau including age, marital status, presence of children, and housing tenure. All of these discrepancies are readily explained by the fact that the telephone sample for Cape Girardeau, purchased from Survey Sampling, Inc., excludes campus housing at Southeast Missouri State University, which is included in the census data used for comparison. As a result, the respondents in our sample are older, less likely to be married or to have children, and more likely to live in owner-occupied housing than the overall Cape Girardeau population as measured by the census. However, our sample may be viewed as quite representative of the great majority of the Cape Girardeau population that does not live in campus housing.

The second discrepancy involves overrepresentation of female respondents, which is typical in telephone surveys. This was not a problem in the

1992 Sikeston sample, but there was modest overrepresentation (7–10 percentage points) in the St. Louis area sample and significant overrepresentation (11–13 points) in the Cape Girardeau sample. However, as this variable has only two categories, we can readily determine the impact, if any, of this overrepresentation of females through cross-tabulations of gender with other variables. If there was any area in which this is likely to have had a substantial effect, it would be Cape Girardeau.

The third exception is that the surveys appear to overrepresent people of higher than average socioeconomic status. For example, in virtually all of the samples, people with less than four years of high school are underrepresented, and those with some college or four years or more of college are overrepresented. Given the relatively higher socioeconomic status of the sample than of the area's population, there may be some tendency to overstate earthquake awareness and preparedness in the survey. However, since correlations of these factors with socioeconomic status are relatively modest, any such bias would be small.

## Awareness of Earthquake Risk

### The Browning Prediction and Earthquake Awareness

Our previous discussions of the Browning prediction focused on the degree to which people believed the prediction, and on how they responded to it behaviorally—either by planning schedule changes or by taking actions to prepare for a possible earthquake. But the prediction also had a significant effect on people's awareness of the earthquake risk facing the New Madrid region over the longer term. As has been noted, there is a significant possibility of an earthquake with a magnitude of around 6.0 to 6.5 in the region during the next decade. The likelihood has been variously placed anywhere between 13 and 63 percent. Chances of such an earthquake during the next fifty years have been placed at anywhere from 50 to 90 percent. To what extent did the Browning prediction help to make the public aware of this risk? We shall begin by discussing perceptions of longer-term earthquake risk as reported in various 1990 and 1991 surveys, then incorporate results from 1992 and 1993 to see to what extent any changes arising from the Browning prediction were sustained.

**1990 and 1991 Survey Results.** In our October 1990 and February 1991 surveys, we asked respondents how likely they thought it was that a damaging earthquake would occur in the next ten to fifteen years. As the top portion of table 4-4 shows, the proportion of people believing that such an earthquake is "very likely" or "somewhat likely" was very high in October 1990, reflecting the public response to the Browning prediction. The effect remained in February 1991, after the prediction was disconfirmed, but there is a notable shift from "very likely," which was the modal response in October, to "somewhat likely," which was the modal response in February. In addition, there is, in Cape Girardeau but not elsewhere, some shift toward the unlikely side of the scale.

**Results from Other Surveys.** As shown in the remainder of table 4-4, a number of surveys by other researchers in the fall of 1990 also asked respondents about the likelihood of a major earthquake over a longer time frame, ranging among various surveys from five years to twenty years (Committee on Preparedness, Awareness, and Public Education, 1993). Consistently, the surveys indicate widespread awareness that the region may experience a damaging earthquake within the next decade or two. The surveys consistently indicate awareness of this risk: 70–85 percent of the respondents in all these surveys said they thought that a damaging New Madrid earthquake was either somewhat likely or very likely during the time period specified in the survey. In fact, some of the surveys show that a sizable portion—perhaps a majority—of respondents actually overestimated the likelihood of a damaging New Madrid quake. In the Wetzel et al. (1991) survey, for example, 12 percent thought that a magnitude 6.3 or greater quake was "certain to happen" by the year 2000, and another 37 percent thought such a quake "very likely." As noted above, the actual probabilities of such a quake in this time frame have been placed at 13 to 63 percent—hardly "certain to happen" and probably not what most statisticians would consider "very likely." Also, about 13 percent of Showalter's (1991) respondents said that there was a 100 percent chance of a magnitude 6.0 or greater quake within the next ten years. Similarly, over half of our October 1990 respondents saw a major quake as "very likely" within the next ten to fifteen years, a percentage that fell to around 35 by February 1991.

Clearly, then, at the time when the Browning prediction was in the news

Table 4-4. Perceived Long-Term Likelihood of a Damaging Earthquake in the New Madrid Fault Zone

| Our Surveys, October 1990 and February 1991 | Likelihood of Major Earthquake Within Next 10–15 Years | | |
|---|---|---|---|
| | | October | February |
| | | (%) | (%) |
| | Very likely | 51.0 | 34.6 |
| | Somewhat likely | 34.9 | 49.8 |
| | Not too likely | 5.5 | 9.3 |
| | Very unlikely | 3.6 | 3.8 |
| | Don't know | 5.0 | 2.4 |

Other Surveys

| Edwards, 1991 | Likelihood of Damaging Earthquake | | |
|---|---|---|---|
| | | In 10 years | In 1 year |
| | | (%) | (%) |
| | Very likely | 29 | 10 |
| | Somewhat likely | 51 | 44 |
| | Not very likely | 18 | 39 |
| | Not likely at all | 3 | 8 |

| Kennedy, 1991 | Likelihood of Major Earthquake in Midwest in Next 5 Years, on Scale of 1 to 10: | |
|---|---|---|
| | | (%) |
| | 7–10 (Very likely) | 22.5 |
| | 4–6 (Somewhat likely) | 48.8 |
| | 1–3 (Not very likely) | 28.8 |

| Levenbach and England, 1991 | Items on likelihood of major earthquake in next 5 years and next 20 years were included in survey but not reported in this paper. |
|---|---|

Table 4-4 continued

| | | |
|---|---|---|
| Showalter, 1991b | Perceived Chance of a Strong (Magnitude 6.0 or Greater) Earthquake in the Region Within the Next 10 Years: | |
| | | (%) |
| | 63–100% chance | 33 |
| | 43–62% chance | 52 |
| | 0–42% chance | 15 |
| Wetzel et al., 1991 | Perceived Chance of a Major (Magnitude 6.3 or Greater) Earthquake in the New Madrid Fault Zone Between 1990 and 2000: | |
| | | (%) |
| | Certain to happen | 12 |
| | Very likely | 37 |
| | Somewhat likely | 30 |
| | Just as likely as not | 17 |
| | Somewhat unlikely | 4 |
| | Very unlikely | <1 |
| | Never will happen | 0 |

and shortly afterward, there was widespread awareness of the long-term earthquake risk in the New Madrid Seismic Zone. There may well have been some tendency to overestimate this risk at the time most of these surveys were taken, though our February survey suggests that more realistic perceptions of the long-term risk may have developed following the Browning "false alarm." Significantly, almost all of the decline in "very likely" responses shifted into the "somewhat likely" category in this survey, and the combined proportion who thought a major quake "very likely" or "somewhat likely" remained almost constant at around 85 percent of those surveyed in both the October and February surveys. There is no doubt from the consistency of these findings that most people in the New Madrid region were aware by late 1990 and early 1991 that the region was at risk for a damaging earthquake. There is little doubt that this awareness was heightened by the series of events including the 1989 Loma Prieta earthquake in the San Francisco Bay area and Browning's pseudoscientific prediction of a December 1990 New Madrid earthquake. For example, a survey conducted in nine communities in the New Madrid Seismic Zone in the mid-1980s had shown a lower level of perceived quake likelihood (Nigg, 1987). At that time, 42 percent had said that there probably or definitely would be a damaging earthquake within the next fifteen years; 46 percent had said there probably or definitely would not. This contrasts with the 1990 and 1991 surveys, in which 70–85 percent of respondents rated a damaging quake as somewhat or very likely. A key question, to which we turn next, is whether this awareness of earthquake risk persisted in the years following the disconfirmation of Browning's prediction.

*Awareness of Earthquake Risk: 1990–1993*

In each of our four surveys, conducted over the 1990–93 period, we asked an identical question concerning how likely the respondent thought it was that a damaging earthquake would occur in the next ten to fifteen years. Figures 4-1, 4-2, and 4-3 show the trend in response to this question for the St. Louis area, Cape Girardeau, and Sikeston between October 1990 and May 1993. Although there is some falloff in the St. Louis area, it is very clear that a large majority of the population throughout the time covered by the four surveys was aware of the risk of a damaging earthquake. A large majority of respondents answered either "very likely" or "somewhat likely" to this question in all three areas at all four points in time. In all areas, the proportion answering "very likely" fell somewhat after the disconfirmation of the Browning prediction, while the proportion answering "somewhat likely" increased. In the 1991, 1992, and 1993 surveys, "somewhat likely" was the most common response in all three areas. It also happens that—with seismologists placing the probability of a magnitude 6.3 earthquake at 13 to 63 percent in the next decade—that is probably the most "correct" answer.

In the St. Louis area, on the one hand, the proportion who thought a damaging quake "not too likely" did increase in 1992 and 1993. By 1993, about 30 percent of the population viewed the possibility of a damaging quake in the next decade as either not too likely or very unlikely. On the other hand, it was still true in May 1993 that more than twice as many St. Louis area respondents—about two-thirds of the total—thought that a damaging earthquake was either somewhat or very likely within the next ten years. The corresponding figures in both Cape Girardeau and Sikeston were even higher, at over 80 percent. In those areas, unlike the St. Louis area, the proportion view-

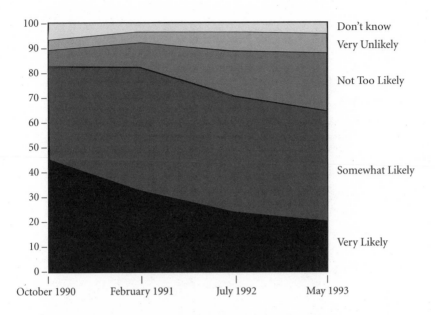

Fig. 4-1. Perceived Likelihood of a Quake, Metro St. Louis Trend, 1990–1993

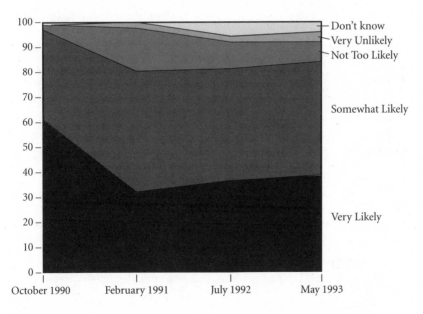

Fig. 4-2. Perceived Likelihood of a Quake, Cape Girardeau Trend, 1990–1993

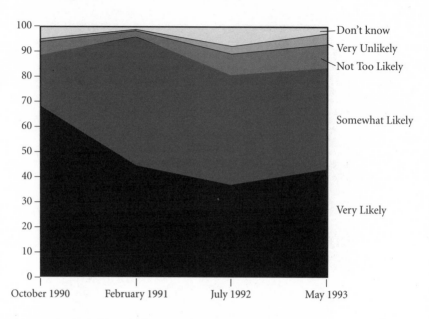

Fig. 4-3. Perceived Likelihood of a Quake, Sikeston Trend, 1990–1993

ing a quake as unlikely did not grow between 1992 and 1993, and it never amounted to more than about 13 percent of survey respondents.

The most pronounced change in the Cape Girardeau and Sikeston areas was a shift from the "very likely" to the "somewhat likely" response after December 1990. There was a smaller and, it turns out, temporary rise in responses on the not-likely side, which appears to have been earlier and more pronounced in Cape Girardeau than in Sikeston. However, that trend did not last: Between 1992 and 1993, there was little change in the proportion of "not likely" responses. In both areas, the percentage giving responses on the "likely" side of the scale rose between 1992 and 1993 because of a decline in "don't know" responses. Thus, unlike the St. Louis area, in Cape Girardeau and Sikeston between 1992 and 1993 earthquake awareness appears to have either held steady or slightly improved. And, despite some falloff in the St. Louis area over the course of the three surveys, our 1993 respondents still chose responses on the likely side of the scale by more than a two-to-one margin. Thus, we conclude that most of the people we surveyed in all three areas continue to see a fair-to-good chance of a damaging earthquake within the next ten to fifteen years. In addition, it appears that much of the gains in awareness that occurred because of the Loma Prieta earthquake and the Browning prediction were still in place two and a half years after that prediction had been disconfirmed.

## Concern about Earthquakes

A different dimension of attitudinal response to earthquake risk is concern. Concern is important because it may be concern, to a greater degree than mere awareness of the risk, that motivates people to action. For example, if people believe that a strong earthquake is likely but they are not concerned about it (perhaps because they think their homes and workplaces are earthquake-proof) they may have little motivation to take actions to prepare for an earthquake.

In our 1990 and 1991 surveys, we did not ask people how concerned they were about the risk of earthquakes in general. The only concern question we asked in those surveys was a retrospective question that we asked in February 1991, a question about how concerned they had been about the possibility of a damaging earthquake in early December 1990. As we reported in chapter 3, the majority stated that they had been only a little or not at all concerned. However, inasmuch as this was a retrospective question and thus subject to poor memory and dissonance reduction bias, and inasmuch as it pertained only to the Browning prediction, it was not in any sense a valid measure of concern about earthquake risk over the longer term. Fortunately, though we did not measure such concern, others did.

### Findings from Other Surveys: Earthquake Concern in 1990 and 1991

In two surveys, in November 1990 and May 1991, Showalter (1993a, 1993b) asked respondents in four small towns in southeast Missouri and northeast Arkansas how concerned they were about the risk of earthquakes. She asked about five kinds of concern: loss of life, injury, property damage, loss of income, and loss of services. She used a scale ranging from 1 (low) to 5 (high), and found mean concern levels ranging from about 3.4 to 4.1 in the November survey and from 2.9 to 3.7 in the May survey. In all cases in the first survey, the modal response was 5; in the second survey it was 3, except for a 5 for loss of services. The highest levels of concern were about property damage and loss of services.

In a survey of Memphis college students, Wetzel et al. (1991) asked two questions that addressed earthquake concern. One involved agreement or disagreement with the statement "I'm scared to death of the possibility of a quake." Approximately 35 percent of their respondents agreed with this statement to some degree, with about half of those agreeing slightly and the rest agreeing or agreeing strongly. These researchers also asked their respondents to what extent they dreamed, daydreamed, or worried about what would happen during an earthquake. They found that 18 percent said they sometimes did, and another 10 percent did so often or very often.

Although the Showalter survey suggests a higher degree of concern than does the Wetzel et al. survey, both show that a sizable number of people in the NMSZ reported some degree of concern about the risk of earthquake. The Showalter survey suggests that the majority of respondents were concerned; the Wetzel et al. survey suggests that about a third were. One possible explanation for this discrepancy is that Showalter's study used a general population survey, whereas Wetzel et al. studied college students.

*Concern in 1992 and 1993*

In our 1992 and 1993 surveys, we asked our respondents how concerned they were about the risk of a damaging earthquake in their community. The responses to these questions are shown in table 4-5. The survey shows that in all three areas we surveyed, the majority were at least somewhat concerned. In fact, "somewhat concerned" is by far the most common of the four choices our respondents were given: It was usually chosen by half or more of them. In Cape Girardeau and Sikeston, the next most common choice was "very concerned"; in those areas, 75–85 percent or more of respondents reported being either very concerned or somewhat concerned. In the St. Louis area, on the other hand, relatively few (around 10 to 15 percent) reported being very concerned; there the combined proportion of very or somewhat concerned respondents was around 60 to 65 percent. In both surveys, around 30 percent said that they were not very concerned, and around 7 percent said that they were not at all concerned. Thus, as with awareness and preparedness, concern about earthquakes was greater in Cape Girardeau and Sikeston, which are closer to the New Madrid fault zone than is St. Louis. There is also evidence of a slight decline in concern between 1992 and 1993, but the difference is small. Moreover, the dominant message is that most people in all three areas remain at least somewhat concerned about the risk of damaging earthquakes, though few are very concerned.

Table 4-5. Earthquake Concern by Geographic Area (July 1992 and May 1993)

| How Concerned Are You about the Risk of an Earthquake? | Cape Girardeau | | Sikeston | | St. Louis Area | |
|---|---|---|---|---|---|---|
| | July 1992 (%) | May 1993 (%) | July 1992 (%) | May 1993 (%) | July 1992 (%) | May 1993 (%) |
| Very concerned | 17.9 | 20.3 | 31.9 | 25.3 | 15.6 | 10.5 |
| Somewhat concerned | 61.3 | 56.3 | 55.9 | 49.8 | 49.8 | 50.3 |
| Not very concerned | 17.0 | 19.4 | 10.0 | 21.0 | 27.4 | 30.9 |
| Not at all concerned | 2.8 | 4.1 | 1.7 | 3.5 | 6.8 | 7.3 |
| Don't know | 0.9 | 0.0 | 0.4 | 0.4 | 0.3 | 0.9 |
| N | 212 | 229 | 229 | 229 | 572 | 673 |

## Trends in Earthquake Preparedness

### 1990–1993 Trends on Three Preparedness Measures

As noted above, there were three preparedness actions about which we asked identical questions in all four surveys. These questions asked whether the respondent had earthquake insurance, had stored canned food and water, and knew how to shut off utilities. In all four surveys we also asked respondents whether they had fastened objects that might fall during an earthquake, but in 1992 and 1993 we asked about the water heater and about "anything else," so that our measure was not strictly comparable across the four surveys.

For the three measures that were strictly comparable in all four surveys, the time trend is shown in figures 4-4, 4-5, and 4-6. The precise pattern varies, but for most actions there is a significant rise between October 1990 and a peak reached in February 1991, followed by a modest decline until July 1992. Then there is a little change or a slight improvement in preparedness between that date and May 1993. For all three preparedness actions in all three geographic areas, the level of preparedness in July 1993 is significantly higher than it was in October 1990. All three preparedness measures were above the 60 percent level everywhere from February 1991 through May 1993.

There were some differences by area. In the St. Louis area, preparedness levels attained in February 1991 were not as high as those attained in the other two areas. However, the St. Louis area also did not have as great a falloff in pre-

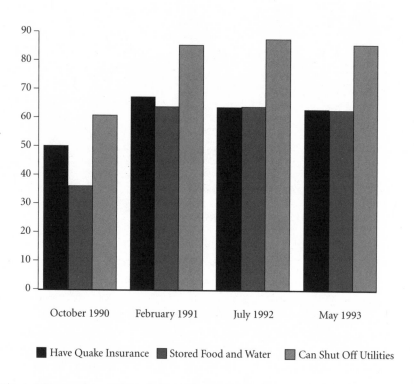

Fig. 4-4. Preparedness, Metro St. Louis Trend, 1990–1993

paredness between 1991 and 1992 as the other two areas did. On the other hand, it also did not experience the partial rebound in several preparedness measures that the other areas experienced between 1992 and 1993.

In all cases, May 1993 preparedness levels for these three actions were similar to or higher than July 1992 levels. Thus for these three actions, it is clear that (1) the Browning prediction stimulated increased preparedness; (2) there was, at most, a modest falloff in preparedness in the year and a half after the prediction was disconfirmed; and (3) after that, there was no further loss in preparedness through mid-1993. We thus conclude that improvements in these preparedness actions resulting from the Browning prediction were for

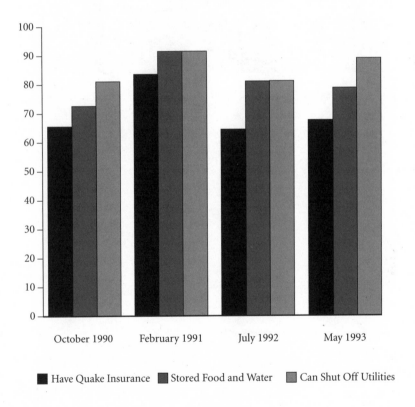

Fig. 4-5. Preparedness, Sikeston Trend, 1990–1993

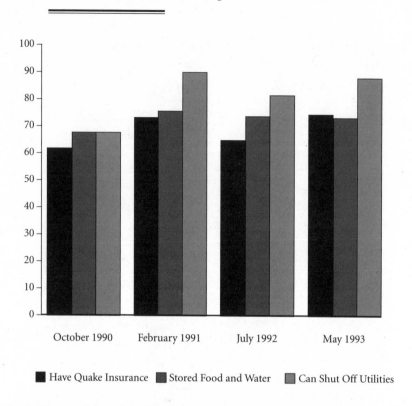

Fig. 4-6. Preparedness, Cape Girardeau Trend, 1990–1993

the most part sustained for at least two and one-half years after the prediction was disconfirmed.

### 1992–1993 Trends on Fourteen Preparedness Measures

Our 1992 and 1993 surveys asked about a broader range of preparedness actions than had our 1990 and 1991 surveys. The results from that part of the survey are shown in table 4-6; the results don't vary much between 1992 and 1993. In general, the findings shown in the table for both years are consistent with

Table 4-6. Objective Preparedness Measures (July 1992 and May 1993)
by Geographic Area

| | Cape Girardeau | | Sikeston | | St. Louis Area | |
|---|---|---|---|---|---|---|
| | July 1992 (%) | May 1993 (%) | July 1992 (%) | May 1993 (%) | July 1992 (%) | May 1993 (%) |
| Stored food or water | 74.3 | 73.9 | 81.2 | 79.0 | 63.8 | 62.7 |
| Earthquake insurance | 65.4 | 74.8 | 64.7 | 67.7 | 63.6 | 61.1 |
| First aid kit | 77.1 | 75.2 | 76.6 | 72.9 | 74.7 | 73.0 |
| Battery radio | 77.1 | 79.3 | 78.3 | 80.8 | 82.2 | 83.2 |
| Safety latches | 29.1 | 18.9 | 26.0 | 17.9 | 26.2 | 18.3 |
| Working flashlight | 95.8 | 95.5 | 96.2 | 95.2 | 95.5 | 95.1 |
| Spare batteries | 65.0 | 75.2 | 68.9 | 77.7 | 75.1 | 75.2 |
| Family quake plan | 43.9 | 44.6 | 49.4 | 36.2 | 32.5 | 29.6 |
| If yes, practiced? | 28.6 | 29.8 | 30.5 | 26.7 | 26.3 | 24.3 |
| Engineer assessed home | 10.4 | 7.7 | 8.9 | 10.0 | 6.8 | 9.5 |
| Made structural changes | 10.9 | 11.3 | 14.0 | 7.0 | 7.8 | 7.9 |
| Fastened water heater | 44.8 | 51.4 | 47.2 | 45.4 | 33.4 | 31.4 |
| Fastened other objects | 20.7 | 24.3 | 25.2 | 20.1 | 16.5 | 13.7 |
| Attended quake meeting | 40.7 | 37.8 | 47.4 | 35.8 | 28.9 | 24.7 |
| Can shut off utilities | 81.8 | 88.6 | 81.3 | 89.1 | 87.1 | 85.4 |
| Mean number of preparedness actions | 7.35 | 7.72 | 7.67 | 7.42 | 6.98 | 6.84 |
| Standard deviation | 2.49 | 2.69 | 2.75 | 2.65 | 2.40 | 2.55 |

what surveys in other earthquake-prone areas have shown: People are more likely to make the easier, less expensive preparations. For the easiest steps, the proportion who took them are strikingly high. In all three areas in both years, approximately three-quarters or more of respondents had a first-aid kit, a battery radio, a working flashlight, and knew how to shut off their utilities. Of course, these are useful preparations not only for an earthquake but also for a wide range of other contingencies. In addition, however, more than 60 percent of respondents in all three areas had earthquake insurance, had stored canned food and water, and had spare batteries on hand for their flashlights and radios.

With respect to the canned food and water, we thought that it would be useful to have some additional information. We were interested in the extent to which people were storing food and water in preparation for an earthquake, as opposed to simply maintaining whatever stocks they might ordinarily keep on their shelves or in their pantry. We were also interested in whether people were replacing their food at least once a year as recommended by earthquake safety agencies. In our May 1993 survey, we asked those who said that they had stored food and water whether the main reason was to prepare for an earthquake. We got different answers in St. Louis and Cape Girardeau/Sikeston. In the St. Louis area, only about 38 percent of those who had stored food and water said that earthquake preparedness was the main reason; in Cape Girardeau and Sikeston, 65 and 73 percent gave that reason. In all three areas, large majorities of those who had stored food and water (74–82 percent) said that they had replaced it within the past year.

For several preparations involving greater effort, the percentages were lower but represented a still substantial minority. These included having a family earthquake plan, fastening the water heater, and having attended an earthquake preparedness meeting. In Cape Girardeau and Sikeston, between a third and a half of respondents indicated that they had done each of these things; in the St. Louis area, around a quarter to a third had done so in both years. In addition, 25–30 percent in all three areas had safety latches on cabinet doors in 1992, although fewer did in 1993. About 25 to 30 percent had actually practiced an earthquake plan in all three areas at the times of both surveys. Between 16 and 25 percent of respondents had fastened other objects besides the water heater, with more having done so in Cape Girardeau and Sikeston than in St. Louis.

While many had taken steps that required a moderate amount of effort, very few had undertaken truly difficult or expensive preparation efforts. One in ten or fewer in all three areas had had an engineer perform an earthquake safety assessment. A similar number said that they had made structural alterations in their homes. However, the extent of these alterations was not determined.

As noted, most preparedness measures showed little change between the 1992 and 1993 surveys, again showing that preparedness was sustained following the Browning prediction. The notable exception to this in all three areas was having safety latches on cabinet doors: Only around 18 or 19 percent had them in 1993, compared to 25 to 30 percent in 1992. Such latches, usually made of plastic, tend to break after a while; perhaps this finding indicates a tendency not to replace them after they do. Some preparedness measures increased between 1992 and 1993, as noted above in our discussion of trends across the four surveys for three preparedness actions. In Cape Girardeau and Sikeston, there were increases in both having spare batteries and knowing how to shut off utilities. Other changes in preparedness, up or down, were modest and isolated. It is clear that consistency, not change, is the dominant feature in comparisons of preparedness actions in 1992 and 1993.

Overall, respondents were asked about fourteen possible preparedness actions. The mean number of affirmative responses was about seven in the St. Louis metropolitan area and between seven and eight in Cape Girardeau and Sikeston. This was true in both 1992 and 1993. While there was little difference among the three areas in the likelihood of taking some actions, such as having a first aid kit or flashlight or knowing how to shut off utilities, there was a more evident geographic pattern for the more difficult steps. In 1992, people in Cape Girardeau and Sikeston—who are closer to the New Madrid fault zone—were more likely to have taken these actions than people in the St. Louis metropolitan area. However, by 1993 this difference was less evident. In all areas, the dominant message is that people did much of what was easy to do to prepare, and most of this preparedness was sustained for at least two and a half years after the Browning prediction had failed to come true.

## Summary and Conclusions: Awareness, Concern, and Preparedness

In this chapter, we have seen that earthquake awareness, concern, and preparedness were all stimulated by Iben Browning's earthquake prediction. As in other areas at risk of earthquake, however, people mostly did what is relatively easy to do to prepare for a damaging earthquake. Our 1992 and 1993 surveys clearly show that the gains in these areas were sustained for at least two and a half years after the disconfirmation of Browning's prediction. Thus, to answer a question we proposed in a paper presentation (Farley, 1994b), a sustained preparedness effect, not a "cry wolf" effect, appears to have been the dominant outcome, at least at the time we studied. This answers one of our key research questions, and in general the findings confirm the first four of the hypotheses outlined at the start of this chapter. The remaining hypothesis has to do with explaining preparedness. In the next chapter, we shall examine the relationship among the three key variables we have measured: earthquake awareness, concern, and preparedness. We shall introduce and analyze some material on earthquake knowledge. In the remaining chapters, we shall use techniques of multivariate analysis to explain what the conditions are that give rise to earthquake awareness, concern, and preparedness.

# 5

# Awareness, Concern, Knowledge, Experience, and Preparedness: Making the Linkages

I N THIS CHAPTER, we shall examine additional aspects of earthquake awareness: knowledge about earthquakes, experience with earthquakes, and perceptions about the consequences of earthquakes. We shall also explore how the three dimensions addressed in the previous chapter—earthquake awareness, concern, and preparedness—are related to one another. To what extent does awareness of earthquake risk lead people to become concerned about earthquakes? To what extent does it stimulate them to become better prepared, or better informed? And what role does concern play in mediating the relationship between awareness and preparedness?

## Knowledge about Earthquakes

### What to Do During an Earthquake

We asked our July 1992 respondents a series of questions about what one should do during an earthquake. They were presented with various actions and asked whether each was a good or a bad thing to do. The proportion giving the correct answer, according to recommendations by safety agencies and preparedness experts, was computed for each item in each geographic area. The results of this analysis appear in table 5-1. The majority gave the correct answer for all actions, but the percentage correct varied from item to item and in some cases also varied by geographic area. Over 90 percent of respondents in all three areas knew that it is a bad idea to get near a window to look out, and a good idea to get under a heavy desk or table. Between 75 and 85 percent

Table 5-1. Knowledge about Good or Bad Actions to Take During an
Earthquake (July 1992)

| What to Do in a Quake | Correct Answer (%) | | |
|---|---|---|---|
| | Cape Girardeau | Sikeston | St. Louis Metro Area |
| Duck and cover | 81.3 | 79.1 | 75.3 |
| Run outside[a] | 75.2 | 72.2 | 65.5 |
| Call police | 69.0 | 66.2 | 67.1 |
| Stand in door or hall[b] | 85.0 | 81.1 | 74.5 |
| Get near window | 97.2 | 95.7 | 95.6 |
| Get under desk or table | 94.8 | 91.8 | 91.0 |

[a]Geographic difference is significant at .05 level.
[b]Geographic difference is significant at .005 level.

knew that it is a good idea to duck down and cover your head or to stand in
a doorway or hallway—but the proportion giving the correct answer on these
items was highest in Cape Girardeau and lowest in the St. Louis area.

The least knowledge was shown on the questions about running outside
or calling the police or fire department for instructions—both considered by
safety experts to be bad ideas. (Running outside is a bad idea because of the
risk of injury from falling objects such as broken glass or building parts. Calling the police or fire department is a bad idea because nonemergency calls
may keep emergency calls from getting through. Also, people should not assume that their phones will work after a major earthquake.) Between 65 and
75 percent knew that these were bad ideas. There was not much geographic
variation on the item about calling the police, but people in the St. Louis area
were less likely than people in the other two areas to know that running outside is not a good idea.

*Can Earthquakes Be Predicted?*

Another aspect of earthquake knowledge of interest to us was people's perceptions, after the Browning fiasco, about the question of whether time- and
place-specific earthquake predictions are possible. We asked about this in both

1992 and 1993. Table 5-2 shows the percentage of respondents agreeing with the statement that "There is no way to predict when an earthquake will occur in any given place." This statement was asked as a way of assessing the extent to which people in the study area may be vulnerable to future pseudoscientific predictions. As table 5-2 indicates, most respondents in both surveys agreed with this statement. Around 80 percent of respondents in Cape Girardeau, 75 percent in Sikeston, and 65 percent in St. Louis agreed or strongly agreed with this statement in the most recent survey.

These figures represent a slight decline between 1992 and 1993 in Sikeston and St. Louis; there was a very slight increase in Cape Girardeau. People are much more likely to "agree" than "strongly agree," but 15–30 percent do "strongly agree" (more than 20 percent did so in four of the six samples). These are relatively large proportions to choose an extreme choice on a Likert scale item with five response choices. The findings clearly suggest that most people in the region are not very vulnerable to future incidents such as the Browning prediction; that event presumably had some "immunization" effect. It suggests also that people may be skeptical in the future of more scientific attempts to predict the time and place of earthquakes, if and when such attempts are made in the New Madrid Seismic Zone.

Table 5-2. Responses to the Statement "There Is No Way to Predict When an Earthquake Will Occur in Any Given Place" (July 1992 and May 1993)

|  | Cape Girardeau | | Sikeston | | St. Louis Metro Area | |
| --- | --- | --- | --- | --- | --- | --- |
|  | July 1992 (%) | May 1993 (%) | July 1992 (%) | May 1993 (%) | July 1992 (%) | May 1993 (%) |
| Strongly agree | 29.4 | 27.9 | 22.1 | 19.7 | 26.3 | 16.6 |
| Agree | 48.1 | 53.2 | 57.0 | 55.5 | 46.9 | 48.4 |
| Disagree | 19.6 | 15.8 | 15.3 | 21.4 | 22.1 | 28.5 |
| Strongly disagree | 1.9 | 1.8 | 3.4 | 2.2 | 3.4 | 3.3 |
| Don't know | .9 | 1.4 | 2.1 | 1.3 | 1.3 | 3.0 |
| N | 214 | 222 | 235 | 229 | 593 | 673 |

## Experience with Earthquakes

In our July 1992 and May 1993 surveys, we asked our respondents whether they had ever "personally experienced an earthquake that caused damage or injuries." If they said yes, we also asked them whether they had suffered damage to their property, and whether they or anyone in their family had been injured. The responses to this question are shown in table 5-3.

Table 5-3. Percentage of Respondents with Experience with Damaging Earthquakes (July 1992 and May 1993 Surveys)

|  | July 1992 | | | May 1993 | | |
|---|---|---|---|---|---|---|
|  | St. Louis Area (%) | Cape Girardeau (%) | Sikeston (%) | St. Louis Area (%) | Cape Girardeau (%) | Sikeston (%) |
| Experienced damaging quake | 26.4 | 32.1 | 25.7 | 14.0 | 23.0 | 15.3 |
| Suffered property damage | 8.7 | 9.7 | 7.5 | 6.9 | 13.4 | 5.7 |
| Respondent or family injured | 2.2 | 2.5 | 2.3 | 1.8 | 2.3 | 0.9 |

This is one of the very few questions for which there appears to be some reliability problem between the 1992 and 1993 surveys. There is little reason to expect a change in people's experience with damaging earthquakes between 1992 and 1993. And the wording and placement of the question in the interview schedule were identical for the two surveys. However, the 1993 experience levels are uniformly lower than those reported in 1992. The percentage reporting that they had experienced a damaging earthquake was about 10 percentage points lower in all three areas. A difference of this magnitude would not occur by chance in samples of the size that were used in St. Louis, where the 95 percent confidence interval was about plus or minus 4 percentage points. It would be unlikely to occur by chance in Cape Girardeau and Sikeston, where the margin of error was about 7 points. Hence, the difference does not appear to be a product of random sampling variation. While the proportion of respondents saying they had experienced a damaging earthquake was lower in 1993 than in 1992, the proportion who said that they personally had suffered damage or injuries as a result of an earthquake was not much different in 1993 than in 1992 in most cases.

It would thus appear that what "counted" as a damaging earthquake was more limited in 1993 than in 1992. This may reflect lesser attention to and concern about the earthquake issue in 1993 than in 1992, but other measures do not indicate a decline of anything like that magnitude. What is clear is that it is perceptual—that is, a matter of what people consider a damaging earthquake, not a change in their actual experiences. This is evident because on the more specific questions about damage and injuries, there is not much change. Whatever may have caused this perceptual change, one thing should be clearly noted: It is not a perceptual change resulting from the Great Flood of 1993, because serious flooding did not occur until after the time at which we conducted the interviews.

Which set of figures regarding experience with damaging earthquakes should be taken more seriously? This is difficult to answer, because what constitutes a "damaging" earthquake is a subjective matter. For example, the September 1990 earthquake shook loose a few wall hangings and was reported to have damaged one house near the epicenter of the quake. Yet throughout most of the region, it caused no damage whatsoever. Thus, it would not be regarded by most people as a "damaging" earthquake, as is evident from our survey responses. Two things are important to keep in mind in discussing the earthquake experiences of residents of the central United States. First, damaging earthquakes are relatively infrequent, and second, net in-migration is relatively low compared with other parts of the country. This limits the chance that residents may have experienced damaging earthquakes where they live now and also ensures that only a small number would have experienced them elsewhere.

The last earthquake in the New Madrid Seismic Zone strong enough to cause widespread damage occurred in 1895; it had a magnitude of 6.2 (Ad Hoc Working Group, 1990). Few if any people who experienced that earthquake would have been alive at the time of our surveys. Earthquakes causing significant localized damage have occurred since then, but not recently. The most recent earthquake in our study area causing any significant damage occurred on November 9, 1968. It was centered near Marion, Illinois, about one hundred miles southeast of St. Louis, and had a magnitude of 5.5. It caused serious damage to a few buildings in St. Louis and minor damage to a number of others, though the damage was not widespread. The most common types of damage were fallen chimneys, broken windows, cracked walls, and damage to loose objects. The press reported one collapsed roof and one collapsed building wall in St. Louis. Windows were broken in several southern Illinois localities, and a cinder block house in southeast Missouri suffered serious damage. There was one serious injury and a few minor ones resulting from falling debris ("Aftershock Followed Earthquake," 1968; "Quake Damage Minor . . . ," 1968; Hopper, 1985).

How many of our respondents might have had memories of this earthquake? In Missouri, the median age of the population in 1990 was 33.5 (U.S. Bureau of the Census, 1992). This would mean that about half of the population would have been alive and ten years old or older at the time of the 1968 earthquake. The majority of our respondents would have been that old by the time of the earthquake, because we surveyed only people who were eighteen or older at the time of the survey. However only a minority would have been adults at the time of the 1968 earthquake. In our 1992 survey, about 75 percent of all respondents were over the age of thirty; in our 1993 sample, about 80 percent were. However, only 33 percent of both our 1992 sample and our 1993 sample were fifty or older. Only those at least forty-five years old would have experienced that earthquake during their adult lives. In addition, most who did experience that earthquake would not have seen any significant damage in their neighborhoods, and some people undoubtedly would not recall an event that long ago. Undoubtedly, some people living in our survey area would have experienced damaging earthquakes in other areas. However, that number is likely to be even smaller. According to the 1990 census, 83 percent of Missouri's population was born in Missouri or elsewhere in the Midwest, and about 95 percent were living in Missouri or elsewhere in the Midwest in 1985 (U.S. Bureau of the Census, 1993). Thus, the percentage likely to have experienced a damaging earthquake anywhere else is certainly small.

What is clear from our data is that most people in our study area reported no experience with damaging earthquakes. Even if we were to use the 1992 figures, the higher of the two surveys, three-fourths of the population in the St. Louis area and Sikeston and two-thirds in Cape Girardeau have had no experience with a damaging earthquake. That is significantly fewer than in California, where even before the destructive Loma Prieta and Northridge earthquakes, many more reported earthquake experience. In the Los Angeles surveys of Turner, Nigg, and Paz (1986), for example, just over half reported having experienced at least one damaging earthquake. This difference is a result of the fact that both felt earthquakes and damaging earthquakes occur much more frequently in California than in the New Madrid region. Moreover, if we go by the more conservative 1993 figures, about six out of seven respondents in the St. Louis area and Sikeston and more than three out of four in Cape Girardeau would have had no experience of a damaging earthquake. By either of our measures, it is safe to say that a large majority of the population of the New Madrid region can recall no personal experience of a damaging earthquake.

The proportion that have suffered either property damage or injury (to themselves or a family member) is even smaller. With one exception (Cape Girardeau in 1993, at 13.4 percent), all of our surveys showed only 5 to 10 percent of respondents reporting that their household had ever suffered damage as a result of an earthquake. And injuries were even less common: Just 1 to 3 percent said that they or anyone in their family had ever been injured as a result of an earthquake. Overall, it is safe to say that only a small minority of the area's population has ever experienced a damaging earthquake and just a tiny proportion have personally suffered damage or injury.

While people in the Midwest have had little experience with damaging earthquakes, they have had considerable experience with other kinds of natural disasters, such as floods and tornadoes. In the first survey conducted in October 1990, we asked our respondents whether they had "ever been the victim of a natural disaster such as a tornado, flood, hurricane, or major earthquake." About a third of the respondents in St. Louis (33.1 percent) and about half in Cape Girardeau and Sikeston (47.5 percent and 52.5 percent, respectively) answered yes. Thus, it appears fair to say that many people in our study region had been personally affected by natural disasters, but, in most cases, they were disasters other than earthquakes. The extent of the earthquake or other disaster experience of our respondents is a significant issue, as past research has linked disaster experience with disaster awareness and preparedness and response to statements about disaster risk. The effects of earthquake experience on awareness, concern, and preparedness in our studies will be examined in later chapters.

## Perceptions of the Consequences of Earthquakes

In an earlier chapter, it was noted that, in the February 1991 survey, a sizable minority of respondents in all three areas believed that many people would be killed and that most buildings in their neighborhoods would collapse if there were a severe earthquake. It was suggested that this may represent an overstatement of the actual consequences of a damaging earthquake, since most neighborhoods—even in very damaging earthquakes, such as Loma Prieta and Northridge—escape without serious damage. Most of the damage is confined to limited areas that have vulnerable buildings, unstable soils, or both. We asked our 1992 and 1993 respondents questions identical to the ones asked in 1991 about the likely consequences of a damaging earthquake in their neighborhoods. Figures 5-1 through 5-6 show the trend across the three surveys in responses to these items.

It is fair to say that if respondents overestimated the consequences in their neighborhoods in the 1991 survey, they did so to an even greater extent in 1992 and 1993. By 1993, about half of all respondents either agreed or strongly agreed that many people would be killed in their neighborhoods. This was the case in all three areas, as shown by figures 5-1 through 5-3. Strong agreement with this item was slightly lower in 1993 than in 1991, but overall agreement was a good deal higher. It rose steadily in Cape Girardeau and Sikeston; in the St. Louis area, most of the increase was between 1991 and 1992.

Even more people thought that most buildings would collapse in their neighborhoods in a severe earthquake. By 1993, a majority agreed that this would happen in all three areas; in Sikeston, nearly two-thirds agreed. Again, this increase was mainly attributable to an increase in the "agree" category, not "strongly agree." But it is a sizable increase nonetheless, since in 1991 only about 40 percent had either agreed or strongly agreed. In St. Louis and Sikeston, most of the increase in agreement with this item occurred between 1991 and 1992; in Cape Girardeau there was a steady increase across the three surveys.

*130*

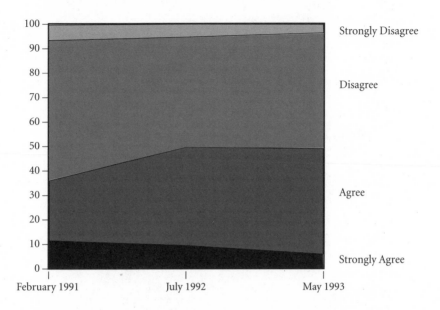

Fig. 5-1. Perceived Likelihood That Quake Would Kill Many, Metro St. Louis Trend, 1990–1993

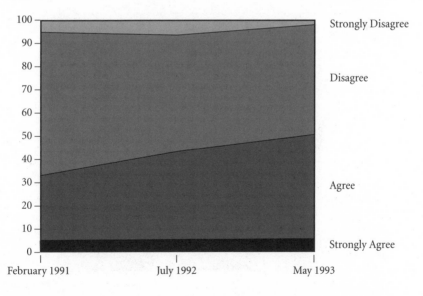

Fig. 5-2. Perceived Likelihood That Quake Would Kill Many, Cape Girardeau Trend, 1990–1993

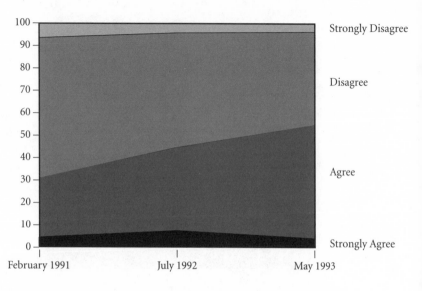

Fig. 5-3. Perceived Likelihood That Quake Would Kill Many, Sikeston Trend, 1990–1993

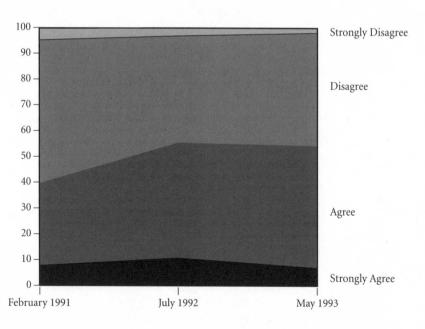

Fig. 5-4. Perceived Likelihood That Buildings Would Fall, Metro St. Louis Trend, 1990–1993

*132*

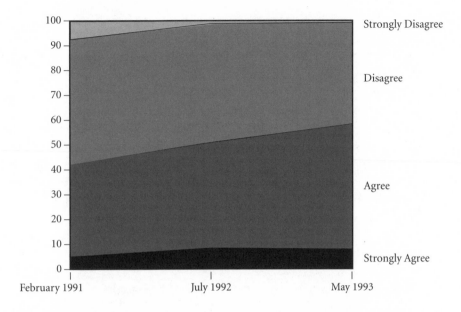

Fig. 5-5. Perceived Likelihood That Buildings Would Fall, Cape Girardeau Trend,
1990–1993

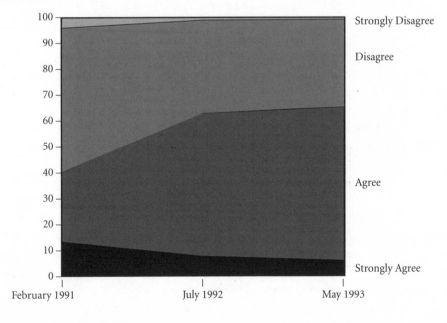

Fig. 5-6. Perceived Likelihood That Buildings Would Fall, Sikeston Trend,
1990–1993

One could, of course, argue that the wording of the question on these items evoked agreement, and that is possibly the case. Respondents may have been reacting to the word "severe," imagining something stronger than the magnitude 6–7 quake most likely to occur. And it may also be that an acquiescent response set accounts for part of the agreement with these items. Neither of these explanations, however, can account for the fact that on both measures in all three areas, the perceived consequences of a damaging earthquake increased. It is possible that the February figures are artificially low—deflated, perhaps, by the disconfirmation of the Browning prediction. Unfortunately, we cannot ascertain this, because we did not ask these questions in the October 1990 survey. But for whatever reason, many people perceive that a severe earthquake would cause major loss of life and serious property damage in their own neighborhoods, and the proportion who feel this way was clearly larger in 1993 than in 1991.

## Linkages among Awareness, Concern, and Preparedness

It is a truism in social research on response to earthquake risk that awareness does not automatically lead to preparedness (Committee on Preparedness, Awareness, and Public Education, 1993; Mileti, Fitzpatrick, and Farhar, 1990; Mileti et al., 1993; Turner, Nigg, and Paz, 1986: 184). For example, perceived risk explained only 2 to 8 percent of the variance in preparedness in Mileti, Fitzpatrick, and Farhar's study (1990: 147) of the Parkfield Earthquake Prediction Experiment. In fact, awareness and perceived risk have generally been shown by past studies to be only weakly related to actual preparedness actions, and to the extent that they are related at all, it is through intermediary variables such as earthquake concern, information-seeking, and perceptions that friends and neighbors are doing something to prepare.

Our findings are consistent with this. We already noted in earlier chapters that there was only a weak relationship between believing the Browning prediction and planning and taking action. This was true both for actions to minimize risk on the days of the predicted earthquake and for actions to prepare for the longer-term risk of earthquakes. We have obtained similar findings regarding the effect of beliefs about the likelihood of a damaging earthquake in the next ten to fifteen years. For example, examine the data in table 5-4. This table, drawn from the May 1993 survey, shows the bivariate relationship be-tween perceived quake likelihood and the number of preparedness actions taken. The analyses show small differences and no consistent relationship be-tween perceived quake likelihood and preparedness, except that those who answered the quake likelihood question "don't know" had taken somewhat fewer preparedness actions than people who were willing to give an assess-ment of quake likelihood, whether high or low. The eta squared figure from the one-way analyses of variance reveals that perceived quake likelihood, even without control for any other variables, explains very little of the variance in the number of preparedness actions taken, 3 to 4.5 percent of the variance in all cases. We also conducted multiple regression analyses of the prepared-ness index in the St. Louis area, Cape Girardeau, and Sikeston in both the 1992 and 1993 surveys. Perceived earthquake likelihood did not emerge as a statistically significant predictor of the preparedness analysis in any of these analyses. We thus conclude that perceived earthquake likelihood—whether short-term or long-term—is only weakly related to taking actions to prepare for an earthquake.

Table 5-4. Mean Number of Preparedness Actions Taken, by Perceived Likelihood of a Damaging Earthquake Within the Next Ten to Fifteen Years (May 1993)

| Perceived Likelihood of a Damaging Quake | Mean Number of Preparedness Actions | | |
|---|---|---|---|
| | Metropolitan St. Louis | Cape Girardeau | Sikeston |
| Very likely | 7.37 | 8.17 | 7.52 |
| Somewhat likely | 7.02 | 7.42 | 7.70 |
| Not too likely | 6.58 | 8.14 | 6.18 |
| Not at all likely | 5.98 | 6.78 | 7.78 |
| Don't know | 5.24 | 6.67 | 5.29 |
| Grand mean | 6.84 | 7.72 | 7.43 |
| Eta squared | .037 | .029 | .045 |
| N of cases | 584 | 200 | 215 |

*Awareness and Concern*

The weak link that does exist between awareness and preparedness may be an indirect one, via the intermediary variable of concern about earthquake risk. As noted in chapter 4, both our 1992 and 1993 respondents and respondents to other surveys in 1990 and 1991 gave responses indicating that many were at least somewhat concerned about the risk of earthquakes. In our surveys, a sizable majority in all three areas in both 1992 and 1993 were at least somewhat concerned. Some past research has identified concern as an intervening variable between awareness and preparedness, while other studies have found concern only weakly related to awareness if at all. Turner, Nigg, and Paz (1986: 158–59), for example, found concern virtually unrelated to awareness, though the measures they used for both concern and awareness were somewhat different from ours. In their study of the Parkfield Earthquake Prediction Experiment, Mileti, Fitzpatrick, and Farhar (1990) treat belief in the prediction and "personalization" of risk as distinct but related dimensions of awareness. The link between concern and action is somewhat better established in the literature, as we shall see.

Our analyses strongly support the notion that there is a weak but nonetheless real relationship between believing that an earthquake is likely and being concerned about the risk of earthquakes. In our 1992 survey, for example, we found correlations ranging from .25 to .35 between perceived quake likelihood and concern about earthquakes in the three geographic areas we studied. Before controls for other variables, these correlations imply that 5–10 percent of the variation in earthquake concern may be accounted for by perceptions about the likelihood of a damaging earthquake in the next ten to fifteen years. And in all three areas, the introduction of control variables did not change this much. Our multivariate analyses indicated that, even after controls for other relevant variables, perceived quake likelihood remained a statistically significant predictor of earthquake concern in all three areas. The beta coefficients between perceived quake likelihood and concern in these regression analyses ranged from .2 to .3 and were highly significant: Significance levels were in all cases .0005 or better. Hence, we conclude that believing that a damaging earthquake is likely in the next ten to fifteen years did lead to increased levels of concern about earthquakes, although the effect is modest.

*Concern and Preparedness*

Does concern lead people to become more prepared? Past studies indicate that it does, but again, the relationships are often weak. Showalter (1993a) found that concern about injury and loss of life was significantly correlated with several individual preparedness measures and with the number of preparedness actions taken. However, the correlations were modest, around .25. Turner, Nigg, and Paz (1986: 188) report a curvilinear relationship between concern and preparedness: Up to a medium-high level of concern, preparedness increased. However, when concern became very high, preparedness fell off. Thus, they conclude that "fear motivates action, but only up to a point" (p. 187). Beyond that point, the dominant effect is paralysis. Nigg (1987) used a similar scale in her survey in the New Madrid region in the mid-1980s. She found a modest positive linear relationship between concern and preparedness, with no evidence of a level of concern above which preparedness fell off.

The Turner, Nigg, and Paz study also found that discussion of earthquake topics was, for many people, the means by which awareness and concern were transformed into action. When people talked with others about what they could do to prepare for a damaging earthquake, they were more likely to take actions. This is similar to findings by Mileti et al. (1993) in their study of public response to an announcement of increased earthquake probabilities in the San Francisco Bay area. They found that seeking additional information about what to do to prepare for an earthquake was the key behavioral link between risk perception and preparedness actions. Risk became personalized through a process of discussing earthquake risk with significant others and searching for published information on how to get ready for an earthquake. When people had done those two things, they were much more likely to take preparedness actions.

To examine the relationship between earthquake concern and earthquake preparedness, we compared the mean number of preparedness actions taken at different levels of concern. This bivariate relationship, from the May 1993 survey, is shown in table 5-5. In all three areas, preparedness increases with concern. The relationship is fairly strong in the St. Louis area and Cape Girardeau, with concern by itself accounting for about 10 and 12 percent of the variation, respectively, in the number of preparedness actions taken. The relationship is weaker in Sikeston, where less than 3 percent of the variance is explained. There is little evidence of the "diminishing returns" pattern noted by Turner, Nigg, and Paz (1986) in their Los Angeles study. In all cases, people who said that they were "very concerned" were better prepared on the average than people who said that they were "somewhat concerned." In this regard, our findings are similar to those obtained by Nigg (1987) in the survey she conducted in the New Madrid region during the mid-1980s.

Table 5-5. Mean Number of Preparedness Actions Taken, by Concern about a Damaging Earthquake in Respondent's Community (May 1993)

| Earthquake Concern | Mean Number of Preparedness Actions | | |
| --- | --- | --- | --- |
| | Metropolitan St. Louis | Cape Girardeau | Sikeston |
| Very concerned | 7.98 | 8.73 | 7.91 |
| Somewhat concerned | 7.22 | 8.04 | 7.41 |
| Not very concerned | 6.41 | 6.10 | 7.17 |
| Not at all concerned | 4.74 | 6.13 | 5.75 |
| Don't know | 5.80 | — | 9.00 |
| Grand mean | 6.84 | 7.72 | 7.43 |
| Eta squared | .096 | .125 | .027 |
| N of cases | 584 | 200 | 215 |

In our findings, the level at which increased concern has the biggest effect on preparedness varies among the three geographic areas, however. In St. Louis and Sikeston, the biggest preparedness gains occurred between the "not at all concerned" and "not very concerned" categories, with the St. Louis area also showing a sizable difference between the "not very concerned" and "somewhat concerned" categories. In Cape Girardeau, in contrast, nearly all of the difference is between the "not very concerned" and "somewhat concerned" categories. Differences occurring higher or lower on the concern scale don't make much difference in preparedness there.

We also included earthquake concern in our multivariate analyses of earthquake preparedness. The findings from these analyses were similar to those described above: The introduction of control variables did not eliminate the relationship between earthquake concern and earthquake preparedness in the St. Louis area and Cape Girardeau. In our multivariate analyses from the May 1993 survey, concern remained a significant predictor of the number of preparedness actions taken in both of these areas after introduction of control variables. The standardized regression coefficients for concern in these analyses were in the .23–.25 range. In Sikeston, however, the relationship was not significant. A similar pattern was also found in multiple regression analyses of the May 1992 data.

Our overall conclusion is that there does appear to be a relationship between concern and preparedness, albeit a modest one. In two of the three areas we studied, this relationship persisted even after controls for other relevant variables. While the Sikeston area stands out as something of an exception in this regard, the overall pattern is consistent with a conclusion that concern does stimulate preparedness. The direct effect of concern on preparedness is clearly greater than that of the perceived likelihood of a quake, although there may be a very small indirect effect of perceived quake likelihood operating through the intermediary variable of quake concern. In other words, people who think an earthquake is likely are somewhat more concerned on average than people who do not, and people who are concerned are somewhat better prepared than people who are not. However, that does not translate into much difference in preparedness between those people who do and those who do not think that a damaging earthquake is likely in the next ten years. This suggests that information telling people why they should be concerned about earthquake risk and information telling people what to do are both likely to stimulate greater earthquake preparedness than information about the likelihood of a damaging New Madrid earthquake.

*Knowledge, Awareness, and Preparedness*

To assess whether people who know more about what to do during an earthquake are better prepared for an earthquake, we examined the correlation between the number of correct answers a respondent gave on the questions about what to do during an earthquake and the number of preparedness actions they had taken. There was no correlation. Knowledge about what to do during an earthquake was also uncorrelated with how likely a person thought a damaging earthquake was to occur, as well as with earthquake concern.

Much the same was true for agreeing with the statement that there is no way to predict when an earthquake will occur in any given place. Agreement with this statement was uncorrelated with the number of preparedness measures taken, as well as with perceived earthquake likelihood, earthquake concern, and knowledge about what to do during an earthquake.

These findings point to two important conclusions. First, one type of knowledge (such as knowing what to do during an earthquake) can and does vary quite independently from other types of knowledge (such as knowledge about the predictability of earthquakes). Second, knowledge by itself does not lead to improved preparedness. This confirms the recommendation in the section above: Mere provision of information will not by itself lead people to prepare. They must see some personal reason for doing so.

As suggested above, correlations of our knowledge measures to other variables were weak. There was, however, one consistent though moderate relationship. In all three geographic areas, there was a statistically significant negative correlation between the index of knowledge about what to do during an earthquake and a belief that "a severe earthquake would kill many people in my neighborhood." As noted earlier, it is not likely that a severe earthquake would kill many people in most neighborhoods; fatalities tend to be concentrated in a limited number of areas with vulnerable construction or unstable soil. In fact, we saw earlier in this chapter that many respondents, especially in the more recent surveys, have overstated the likely consequences of a major earthquake in their neighborhoods. Thus, what is likely occurring here is a correlation between two types of knowledge about earthquakes: knowledge of what to do when one occurs and a reasonable expectation of the consequences. Recall, however, that while these types of knowledge do correlate, others, such as knowing what to do during an earthquake and knowing that the specific time and place of earthquakes cannot be predicted, do not.

## Summary and Conclusions

In this chapter, we have examined the level of knowledge about earthquakes of our respondents and the relationships among knowledge, awareness, concern, and preparedness. We have seen that most people have a reasonably good knowledge of what to do during an earthquake and most understand that the time and place of an earthquake cannot be predicted. Although there were differences in responses to the 1992 and 1993 survey, it is clear that a large majority of our survey respondents had no experience with damaging earthquakes and that only a tiny fraction had experienced injury or property damage as a result of an earthquake. Our respondents in many cases overestimated the likely consequences of a damaging New Madrid earthquake, and this tendency appears to have increased since 1991. There appears to be no direct link between perceptions about the likelihood of a damaging earthquake and earthquake preparedness, but there may be an indirect link via earthquake concern. Those who think a damaging earthquake is likely tend to be somewhat more concerned about earthquake risk, and those who are more concerned are somewhat better prepared. We shall now explore further what factors give rise to earthquake awareness, concern, and preparedness through use of multivariate analysis of our 1992 and 1993 surveys.

# 6

# Explaining Awareness and Concern

W E CONDUCTED MULTIVARIATE ANALYSES of our awareness, concern, and preparedness measures in order to determine the factors contributing to each. The technique used in these analyses was multiple regression. We performed multiple regressions using data from both the July 1992 and May 1993 surveys and, for some analyses, the October 1990 survey also. The fact that we conducted multiple surveys with many identical variables enabled us to examine the extent to which the predictors influencing awareness, concern, and preparedness remained persistent over time.

We began our multivariate analyses by including a variety of predictors in the regression models. We felt there was a reasonable theoretical basis for believing that each of the predictors included might have an influence upon the dependent variable. The predictors included attitudinal, experiential, perceptual, behavioral, and sociodemographic factors. Typically, these initial models included around ten to fifteen predictor variables. In all cases, some of these predictors proved to be statistically related to the dependent variable, while others did not. After these initial analyses, we performed more limited analyses including only those variables shown by the initial analysis to be statistically related to the dependent variables. These are the regression analyses reported in this and subsequent chapters; however, in all cases we also present tables showing the predictor variables that were included in the initial analysis. In general, the variables included in the more limited analyses were ones that had statistically significant relationships with the dependent variable in the initial relationship, or ones in which the relationship approached statistical significance, generally meaning p <.10 in the St. Louis area samples or p <.20 in the smaller Cape Girardeau and Sikeston samples.

## Explaining Perceived Earthquake Likelihood

The predictors we included in our initial analysis of respondents' perceptions about the likelihood of a damaging earthquake in the next ten to fifteen years are shown in table 6-1. We performed these regression analyses using data from the 1992 and 1993 surveys and also the 1990 survey. The 1992 and 1993 surveys included certain items not included in the earlier surveys, while the 1990 survey offers an opportunity to assess the effects of response to the Browning prediction on perceptions about the longer term risk of damaging earthquakes.

In the analyses of the 1990 data, we included most of the same predictors we had used in our analysis of people's belief in the Browning prediction, with the addition of that belief itself. We wanted to see what effect believing the Browning prediction had had on people's perceptions about the long-term likelihood of a damaging earthquake in the region. We also wanted to see whether the factors we had identified as having effects on believing Browning's prediction had either direct effects on the perceived long-term likelihood of an earthquake, or indirect effects through their effects on believing Browning.

In the 1992 and 1993 surveys, the items we added were measures assessing trust in science and in other sources of information, self-assessed and actual earthquake knowledge, and earthquake experience. Our research and that of others suggested to us that perceptions about science, specifically including trust versus distrust of science, are likely to influence responses to both pseudoscientific or nonscientific earthquake predictions and scientific statements and predictions, such as scientific statements about the probabilities of an earthquake of various magnitudes in the New Madrid fault zone during the coming decade. We also replaced the general disaster experience measure used in the 1991 survey with a more specific measure of earthquake experience. We retained the same sociodemographic variables we had used in the 1990 and 1991 analyses.

The findings from the 1990 survey are shown in table 6-2, while the findings from the 1992 and 1993 surveys are presented in table 6-3. It turns out that the best immediate predictor of people's views in 1990 about the long-

Table 6-1. Predictors Included in Initial Analysis of the Perceived Likelihood of a Damaging Earthquake Within the Next Ten to Fifteen Years

July 1992 and May 1993 Surveys

Attitudinal Issues
    Trust in what scientists say about things I don't understand*
    Trust in what religious leaders say about things I don't understand*
    Perception that time and place of earthquake cannot be predicted
Experiential Issues
    Experienced damaging earthquake
Perceptual Issues
    Self-assessed knowledge about earthquake preparedness
Sociodemographic Issues
    Gender
    Race
    Age group
    Educational level
    Household income
    Presence of children under 18
    Own or rent housing

*Asked in 1992 survey only.

October 1990 Survey

Attitudinal Issues
    Likelihood of war with Iraq
    Likelihood of December 1990 earthquake
    September quake caused change in thinking on December quake likelihood
Experiential Issues
    Been victim of natural disaster
Perceptual Issues
    Scientists good source of earthquake information
Behavioral Issues
    Discussed Browning forecast with others
Sociodemographic Issues
    Gender
    Race
    Age group
    Educational level
    Household income
    Presence of children under 18
    Marital status

term likelihood of an earthquake was what they thought about the likelihood that Browning's predicted earthquake would occur. Other than that one relationship, our predictors did a rather poor job of pinpointing those who thought that an earthquake was likely over the next ten to fifteen years. It is notable which factors did not correlate strongly to people's beliefs about the likelihood of an earthquake in the next ten to fifteen years. We had thought that education, income, marital status, earthquake experience, and trust in what scientists say about things the respondent does not understand were all variables that might be related to perceived earthquake likelihood. Better educated people, for example, might be more aware that scientists say that a damaging earthquake is a good possibility. People who trust what scientists say might pay more attention to scientific pronouncements. Married people and people with a higher income might have a greater personal stake in paying attention to statements about a natural hazard that can cause death, injury, and property damage. In reality, however, those predictors were only weakly if at all related to belief in the likelihood of an earthquake in the next ten years, not of any effect of one's reaction to the Browning prediction. Although many predictors had little or no effect on people's perceptions about earthquake likelihood, there are nonetheless some meaningful inferences that can be drawn from the data, particularly by comparing our 1990 results to what we found in 1992 and 1993.

*Findings from the 1990 Survey*

Table 6-2 shows 1990 survey results.Because sample sizes were smaller than in the later surveys and because there is a need in regression for listwise deletion of cases with missing data, the $N$s are smaller for the regression analyses in the 1990 survey than in the later surveys and also smaller than for univariate and bivariate tables from the 1990 survey. Hence, we report regression analyses for the entire sample for which data were available on all variables listed in table 6-1 ($N = 326$), for the St. Louis metropolitan area ($N = 226$), and for a combined Cape Girardeau/Sikeston Sample ($N = 100$). Keep in mind that the regressions shown here utilize only a subset of the variables listed in table 6-1. All of the variables in table 6-1 were included in initial regression analyses not reported here; here we report analyses including only the predictors these initial analyses identified as being sufficiently related to the dependent variable to attain or approach the .05 level of statistical significance.

Table 6-2. Regression Analysis of the Perceived Likelihood of a Damaging Earthquake Within the Next Ten to Fifteen Years (October 1990)

| | Combined Sample | | | | St. Louis Area | | | | Cape Girardeau/Sikeston | | | |
|---|---|---|---|---|---|---|---|---|---|---|---|---|
| | Model 1 | | Model 2 | | Model 1 | | Model 2 | | Model 1 | | Model 2 | |
| | B | Beta | B | Beta | B | Beta | B | Beta | B | Beta | B | Beta |
| Scientists good information source | .329 | .203[c] | .174 | .103[a] | .291 | .170[b] | .167 | .098 | .429 | .340[d] | .230 | .182 |
| Likelihood of war with Iraq | .169 | .117[a] | .096 | .066 | .214 | .137[a] | .105 | .067 | | | | |
| Gender* | .211 | .146[b] | .092 | .064 | .223 | .144[a] | .105 | .068 | .213 | .193[a] | .096 | .087 |
| Age | -.180 | -.227[f] | -.124 | -.180[e] | -.179 | -.220[d] | -.136 | -.167 | -.156 | -.225[a] | -.133 | -.193[a] |
| Income | .068 | .090 | .066 | .087 | .085 | .106 | .071 | .089 | | | | |
| Education | -.103 | -.133[a] | -.055 | -.071 | -.113 | -.132 | -.058 | -.069 | -.063 | -.112 | -.034 | -.060 |
| Race† | | | | | | | | | .227 | .158 | .257 | .178 |
| Children under 18 | | | | | | | | | -.137 | -.128 | -.096 | -.090 |
| Likelihood of December quake | | | .275 | .378[f] | | | .286 | .377[f] | | | .195 | .316[c] |
| Discussed Browning forecast | | | .392 | .153[c] | | | .410 | .158[a] | | | .307 | .136 |
| $R^2$ | .151 | | .304 | | .153 | | .301 | | .198 | | .306 | |
| Adjusted $R^2$ | .136 | | .286 | | .130 | | .275 | | .146 | | .245 | |
| F | 9.491 | | 17.284 | | 6.603 | | 11.684 | | 3.812 | | 5.022 | |
| Significance | .0001 | | .0001 | | .0001 | | .0001 | | .005 | | .0001 | |
| N | 326 | | 326 | | 226 | | 226 | | 100 | | 100 | |

*Positive coefficient indicates that females consider quake to be more likely.
†Positive coefficient indicates that whites consider quake to be more likely.

[a]Significant at .05 level.
[b]Significant at .01 level.
[c]Significant at .005 level.
[d]Significant at .001 level.
[e]Significant at .0005 level.
[f]Significant at .0001 level.

*146*

The columns labeled "Model 1" include predictors unrelated to the Browning prediction. In the columns labeled "Model 2," the perceived likelihood of the quake predicted by Browning and a variable indicating whether the respondent had discussed the Browning prediction with significant others are added to the model. Model 1 explains 13–15 percent of the variance in perceived quake likelihood. In both the St. Louis area and the Cape Girardeau /Sikeston areas, women, younger people, and people with lower levels of education perceive an earthquake to be more likely in the next ten to fifteen years. One attitude we measured is also correlated to perceived quake likelihood in both areas: rating scientists as a good source of information about earthquakes. In St. Louis but not Cape Girardeau/Sikeston, the perceived likelihood of a war with Iraq was also correlated with the perceived likelihood of an earthquake within ten to fifteen years. In Cape Girardeau/Sikeston but not the St. Louis area, whites and people with no children under eighteen saw a damaging earthquake in the next ten years as somewhat more likely than did people of color and people with children, respectively. These two relationships approach but do not quite reach the .05 significance level, but keep in mind the relatively small size of the Cape Girardeau/Sikeston sample (one hundred) in this survey. Because the relationship is not statistically significant, we cannot conclude that race or the presence of children had any effect on perceptions about earthquake risk, but the possibility is worth further investigation in future studies.

When we added two variables related to the Browning prediction to the model, the results were quite different (Model 2 in table 6-2). The proportion of explained variance rose to the .25–.3 range, and the best predictor of perceived likelihood of a damaging earthquake in the next ten to fifteen years was how likely the respondents thought one was on December 2 or 3, 1990. Another significant predictor of perceived likelihood of a quake in the next ten to fifteen years was whether respondents had discussed the predicted December earthquake with their friends, neighbors, and relatives. Those who had discussed the prediction with significant others were more likely to think that there would be a damaging earthquake within the next ten to fifteen years. Thus, believing the Browning prediction and, independent of that, talking about it with others, were the best predictors of people's beliefs about the likelihood of a damaging earthquake over the longer run.

The latter is supportive of findings by Turner, Nigg, and Paz (1986), Mileti and Fitzpatrick (1993), and Mileti et al. (1993) that discussion of earthquake predictions with significant others is an important part of the process by which people formulate their response to earthquake predictions. It suggests that when people discussed Browning's earthquake prediction, it helped them to become aware of the longer-term risk of earthquakes in the New Madrid Seismic Zone. These findings are also consistent with the two-step flow of communication theory discussed earlier: Discussions with significant others are an important means by which people decide what meaning to give to information they receive from the mass media.

The finding that discussion of the Browning prediction had a significant effect on the perceived long-term likelihood of damaging earthquakes is particularly significant in light of one other finding: Discussing the Browning prediction was not correlated (in either direction) with believing the Browning prediction. Apparently, when people discussed the prediction, they were not led either to believe it or disbelieve it, but discussion of it does seem to have been a mechanism by which people became aware of the longer-term risk of damaging earthquakes in the New Madrid region.

Another important finding is that the introduction of the two variables related to Browning eliminated the effects that most of the other significant predictors had in Model 1. Only age and the belief that scientists are a good source of information about earthquakes continued to have significant effects on the perceived likelihood of a quake within ten to fifteen years. Thus, it would seem that some of the predictors—notably gender, education, and the expectation of war—influenced views about the long-term likelihood of an earthquake only because they influenced the extent to which people believed that Browning's predicted earthquake would occur. Outside the Browning context, they may have little to do with people's perceptions about the likelihood of a damaging earthquake.

There is, it should be noted, an alternative interpretation. One could argue that our regression models place the variables in the wrong causal order: that some people believe that the New Madrid fault zone carries the potential for damaging earthquakes, and those are the people who believed Browning. There is no statistical way to test this, since a plausible theoretical argument could be made for either causal order. We doubt that the causal order we have proposed is wrong, however. Were that the case, variables that influence the perceived long-term likelihood of an earthquake before controls for reactions to Browning ought to continue to do so after controls. Most of them do not. More to the point, if the causal order were the opposite of what we have proposed, the predictors that influence the perceived long-term likelihood of a quake in the Browning context ought also to do so outside the Browning context, in 1992 and 1993. As we shall see in greater detail shortly, that is not the case at all for some predictors (such as education), and it is true only to a limited extent for others (such as gender). Hence, we conclude that the most likely causal order is the one we have modeled in our regression analysis, in which response to and discussion of the Browning prediction led people to think more about the long-term earthquake risk. This is also consistent with our findings that, during and after the time of the Browning prediction, the perceived likelihood of a damaging earthquake within the next ten to fifteen years was at a higher level than had been measured by Nigg (1987) several years before the Browning prediction.

*Findings from the 1992 and 1993 Surveys*

The regression analyses of perceived earthquake likelihood in the ten to fifteen after the 1992 and 1993 surveys are shown in table 6-3. Again, this table reports only those predictors that had a significant or near-significant effect on the perceived likelihood of a quake, although preliminary analyses were run with all the variables shown in the applicable part of table 6-1. There are a number of differences between the variables used in the 1992 and 1993 analyses and those used in the 1990 analysis. First, a number of items in the 1990 analysis are absent in 1992 and 1993 because they pertained to the Browning prediction, the minor earthquake in September 1990, or the anticipation of the Gulf War. None of those factors were applicable in 1992 and 1993.

Second, the item regarding science was changed from an assessment of scientists as a source of earthquake information to a global measure of trust in scientists. This item had been changed in the 1991 survey in order to test a hypothesis that people who had believed Browning distrusted institutions such as science, and it was part of a scale measuring attitudes toward other institutions as well (such as government and religion). We decided to keep this scale in the 1992 survey, and the items on scientists and religious leaders appear in table 6-1 (because they turned out to lack much predictive power, they were dropped from the 1993 survey, however).

Third, the disaster experience item in the 1990 survey was changed to an earthquake experience item in the 1992 and 1993 surveys, so as to assess the effects of experience with that type of disaster specifically. Fourth, we added two new items in 1992: a self-assessment of knowledge about earthquake preparedness, and a question on whether the time and place of earthquakes can be predicted (as noted in chapter 5, this was used as a measure of earthquake knowledge).

Table 6-3. Regression Analysis of the Perceived Likelihood of a Damaging Earthquake Within the Next Ten to Fifteen Years (July 1992 and May 1993)

| | St. Louis Area | | | | Cape Girardeau | | | | Sikeston | | | |
|---|---|---|---|---|---|---|---|---|---|---|---|---|
| | July 1992 | | May 1993 | | July 1992 | | May 1993 | | July 1992 | | May 1993 | |
| | B | Beta | B | Beta | B | Beta | B | Beta | B | Beta | B | Beta |
| Can't predict when quake will occur | | | | | -.053 | -.065 | Analysis Not Reported: No Significant Predictors | | | | Analysis Not Reported: No Significant Predictors | |
| Earthquake experience | .249 | .127[c] | .213 | .082 | | | | | | | | |
| How much know about preparedness | | | | | | | | | .050 | .077 | | |
| Gender* | .230 | .129[c] | .216 | .120[b] | .160 | .104 | | | .305 | .187[b] | | |
| Age | -.121 | -.130[c] | | | -.150 | -.190[b] | | | | | | |
| Marital status† | | | .053 | .075 | .223 | .147[a] | | | .104 | .064 | | |
| Income | | | -.092 | -.105[a] | | | | | .120 | .145 | | |
| | | | | | | | | | | | | |
| $R^2$ | | .044 | | .042 | | .057 | | | | .074 | | |
| Adjusted $R^2$ | | .039 | | .035 | | .037 | | | | .055 | | |
| F | | 8.404 | | 5.826 | | 2.870 | | | | 3.847 | | |
| Significance | | .0001 | | .0001 | | .05 | | | | .005 | | |
| N | | 546 | | 540 | | 196 | | | | 198 | | |

*Positive coefficient indicates that females consider quake to be more likely.
†Positive coefficient indicates that married people consider quake to be more likely.

[a]Significant at .05 level.
[b]Significant at .01 level.
[c]Significant at .005 level.

It turns out that the 1992 and 1993 models had less predictive power than the ones we had used in 1990—even the 1990 model that did not include variables related to Browning. Whether this is because of the different variables used, the waning influence of the Browning prediction, or some other reason is not clear. Our 1992 models explain only about 3 to 6 percent of the variance in the perceived likelihood of a damaging earthquake, and the 1993 models even less. In fact, analyses for Cape Girardeau and Sikeston are not reported because neither any predictor nor the analysis as a whole was statistically significant. Although the relationships are weak, a few consistent patterns appear. In general, women see a damaging earthquake in the next ten to fifteen years as more likely than men. That is true in varying degrees in all three geographic areas in 1992 and in St. Louis in 1993. This finding is similar to those of previous studies. Less consistently, younger people and married people see a damaging earthquake as more likely. In St. Louis only, people with experience of a damaging earthquake see it as more likely than those without experience. As noted, however, all of these relationships are weak. Outside the Browning context, and with the variables we included in our 1992 and 1993 analyses, perceived earthquake likelihood is difficult to explain.

*Two Suggestions for Future Research*

The different performance of our 1990 and 1992/93 analyses leads us to two suggestions for future research on perceptions about the likelihood of natural disaster. In retrospect, it appears that we may have measured certain variables relevant to perceived earthquake likelihood better in the 1990 survey than in the more recent ones. That is in part because in the context of events occurring in the fall of 1990, they were easier to measure. The Browning prediction, the minor earthquake of September 26, and the Iraqi invasion of Kuwait and the resultant buildup for the Gulf War all stimulated concern and uneasiness in the region's population. We have suggested elsewhere that generalized fear about various dangers may have been a key factor in how people responded to Browning's prediction. We believe that such generalized fear may be one reason for the correlation between believing Browning's prediction and believing in the fall of 1990 that what turned out to be the Gulf War would occur. Significantly, the regressions reported in table 6-2 indicate that believing that war with Iraq was likely had at least an indirect effect on people's perceptions about the longer-term likelihood of a damaging earthquake. We had no measure similar to our Iraq war question in the 1992 or 1993 surveys, mainly because no threat of war loomed then. Consequently, we had no variable that could measure generalized fears and concerns the way the war variable had done in the earlier surveys. In light of the better performance of the 1990 models than the 1992 and 1993 models, we suggest that measures of generalized fear and concern be added to future studies of people's beliefs about the likelihood of natural disasters.

We also found in the 1990 survey that viewing scientists as a good information source was a good predictor of people's perceptions about the likelihood of a damaging earthquake—and in some cases it remained so even after belief in Browning's prediction was added to the model. Significantly, viewing scientists as a good source of information about earthquakes was highly correlated to viewing government and business as good sources of information about earthquakes. Moreover, as discussed in chapter 2, all three of these predictors correlated positively with beliefs that the December earthquake would occur as predicted. We interpreted that finding as a product of the effect of skepticism or lack thereof. People who see one source of information as good see others as good—even if the sources are different and put out different information.

Moreover, people who saw these sources of information as good were more likely to believe Browning. They were, in short, unskeptical—about Browning, about science, about government, and about business. Table 6-2 tells us that this unskeptical attitude was positively correlated with perceptions that a damaging earthquake in the next ten to fifteen years is likely. It has indirect effects via acceptance of the Browning prediction, and in the combined sample, at least, appears to have direct effects as well. Apparently because we replaced this item in the 1992 survey with one worded in a way that emphasized trust rather than a rating of information sources, we were not able to detect an effect of this type in the more recent survey. All of this leads us to suggest that a generalized measure of skepticism—focusing on believing or not believing what one hears from a variety of sources—ought to be included in future studies about the perceived likelihood of natural disasters. We propose that the unskeptical person may think, "Yes it will happen, just as they say," whereas the more skeptical person may think, "It's not really going to happen; they have no way to know that it will."

## Explaining Concern about Earthquakes

The predictors used in our multivariate analyses of concern about earthquakes are shown in table 6-4. These analyses included the same predictors used in the 1992 and 1993 analyses of the perceived likelihood of a quake, but several things were added. First, the perceived likelihood of a damaging earthquake is itself a strong candidate as a significant predictor of concern. People are not

Table 6-4. Predictors Included in Initial Analysis of Concern about the Risk of a Damaging Earthquake (July 1992 and May 1993)

Attitudinal Issues
  Trust in what scientists say about things I don't understand*
  Trust in what religious leaders say about things I don't understand*

Efficacy Issues
  Think that preparations for earthquake will work
  Think that quakes will cause loss of life no matter what

Experiential Issues
  Experienced damaging earthquake

Perceptual Issues
  Likelihood of damaging earthquake within next ten to fifteen years
  Self-assessed knowledge about earthquake preparedness
  Perception that time and place of earthquake cannot be predicted
  Think that severe earthquake would kill many people in neighborhood
  Think most buildings in neighborhood would collapse in severe earthquake
  Think that neighbors would have no idea what to do in an earthquake

Sociodemographic Issues
  Gender
  Race
  Age group
  Educational level
  Household income
  Presence of children under 18
  Marital status
  Own or rent housing

*Asked in 1992 survey only.

apt to be concerned about an event they do not think will happen. Second, we also added as predictor variables several perceptual items regarding what would happen in a damaging earthquake in the respondent's neighborhood. In short, how personally at risk do people feel in their own neighborhoods? As noted earlier, personalization of risk appears to be an important step in developing concern about and preparedness for damaging earthquakes.

These predictors include beliefs that in a severe earthquake, many people would be killed in the respondent's neighborhood, that most buildings in the neighborhood would collapse, and that most neighbors would have no idea what to do. These items were preceded by a brief introduction asking the respondent the following: "Think about the neighborhood you live in, especially the five or six blocks around your home." The idea was to make the sense of risk personally relevant. Third, we added two measures of a continuum that might be labeled as efficacy at one end and fatalism at the other. These were Likert-type items, one stating, "If I make preparations for an earthquake, I am almost certain that they will work"; the other said, "I believe that earthquakes are going to cause widespread loss of life and property whether we prepare for them or not." Both of these items are replications of items used by Turner, Nigg, and Paz (1986) to measure the fatalism/efficacy continuum in their Los Angeles surveys. Their research clearly showed that fatalism was an important predictor of earthquake preparedness; we included it in this part of the analysis to see whether and how it may also relate to concern that can stimulate preparedness.

As can be seen in table 6-5, our models do better at explaining concern than at explaining the perceived likelihood of a quake. The adjusted $R^2$ values range from around .10 to .26 in our analyses of earthquake concern, averaging about .18. The most variance explained, 18–26 percent, is in Cape Girardeau. In both 1992 and 1993, the models explained between 15 and 16 percent of the variance in the St. Louis area. They performed least well in Sikeston, explaining 10–12 percent of the variance there.

*Earthquake Awareness and Earthquake Concern*

As noted in chapter 5 in our discussion of the relationship between earthquake awareness and earthquake concern, there is a consistent, statistically significant relationship between the perceived likelihood of a damaging earthquake in the next ten to fifteen years and concern about earthquakes. This was evi-

Table 6-5. Regression Analysis of Earthquake Concerns (July 1992 and May 1993)

| | St. Louis Area | | | | Cape Girardeau | | | | Sikeston | | | |
|---|---|---|---|---|---|---|---|---|---|---|---|---|
| | July 1992 | | May 1993 | | July 1992 | | May 1993 | | July 1992 | | May 1993 | |
| | B | Beta | B | Beta | B | Beta | B | Beta | B | Beta | B | Beta |
| Quake likelihood | .224 | .239$^f$ | .290 | .341$^f$ | .205 | .270$^e$ | .242 | .262$^e$ | .255 | .278$^f$ | .295 | .302$^f$ |
| Preparation will work | .228 | .190$^f$ | .117 | .086$^a$ | .158 | .152$^a$ | .332 | .265 | .120 | .110 | | |
| Buildings would fall in neighborhood | .091 | .081 | | | .155 | .186$^a$ | | | | | | |
| Quake would kill in neighborhood | .064 | .117$^b$ | .185 | .163$^f$ | | | | | | | | |
| Can't predict time and place of quake | | | .059 | .060 | | | | | | | | |
| Earthquake experience | | | -.149 | -.068 | | | | | | | | |
| Neighbors don't know what to do | | | | | -.093 | -.269$^e$ | | | | | | |
| Quakes will cause loss no matter what | | | | | .142 | .171$^a$ | .185 | .167$^a$ | | | | |
| Trust scientists | | | | | | | | | .028 | .057 | | |
| Trust religious leaders | | | | | | | | | .031 | .100 | | |
| Education | -.195 | -.109$^a$ | | | | | | | .027 | .038 | | |
| Income | | | | | -.115 | -.202$^b$ | | | | | | |
| Race* | | | -.133 | -.075 | | | .207 | .105 | | | .291 | .127 |
| Presence of children | | | | | .164 | .142$^a$ | | | | | | |
| Marital status† | | | | | | | .055 | .094 | | | | |
| Gender†† | | | | | | | | | | | .220 | .130$^a$ |
| $R^2$ | .160 | | .166 | | .297 | | .207 | | .133 | | .129 | |
| Adjusted $R^2$ | .152 | | .156 | | .264 | | .185 | | .099 | | .116 | |
| F | 18.496 | | 17.140 | | 9.062 | | 9.440 | | 3.928 | | 10.441 | |
| Significance | .0001 | | .0001 | | .0001 | | .0001 | | .0005 | | .0001 | |
| N | 490 | | 523 | | 158 | | 187 | | 188 | | 216 | |

*Positive coefficient indicates that people of color more concerned.
†Positive coefficient indicates that married people more concerned.
††Positive coefficient indicates that females more concerned.

$^a$Significant at .05 level.
$^b$Significant at .01 level.
$^c$Significant at .005 level.
$^d$Significant at .001 level.
$^e$Significant at .0005 level.
$^f$Significant at .0001 level.

dent in all three areas in both surveys. The standardized regression coefficients (beta coefficients) for this predictor are consistently between .24 and .34. That confirms what we said in chapter 5: There is a consistent and significant, if modest, effect of the perceived likelihood of a quake on concern, and it persists even when other relevant variables are held constant. While awareness (as measured by the perceived likelihood of a quake) and concern are clearly two different things, it is equally clear that they are related. The more likely a person thinks a damaging earthquake is, the more concerned that person is apt to be.

## Efficacy and Earthquake Concern

There is also a consistent effect of one of our efficacy measures: the belief that preparations for an earthquake will work. In four of our six samples (the St. Louis area and Cape Girardeau in both 1992 and 1993), this relationship is statistically significant, and in a fifth (Sikeston in 1992) it approaches statistical significance. In all five cases, people who are "almost certain" that their preparations will work are more concerned about earthquakes. Concern, it seems, is highest among people who perceive that there is a risk and that they can do something about it. It is not irrational fear, but rather an empowered response to an understood risk. In contrast, people who do not believe that their preparations will work report lower levels of concern, even if their belief in the likelihood of a quake is just as great as that of their neighbors. For those who do not think that preparation would work, being concerned about an earthquake could raise feelings of cognitive dissonance or heightened powerlessness: "There is a real risk, but I can't do anything about it." Hence, they seemingly put it out of their minds.

## Earthquake Consequences and Earthquake Concern

We found somewhat less consistent, but often statistically significant, relationships between measures of perceived earthquake consequences and earthquake concern. Those who perceived greater consequences in their neighborhood tended to report higher levels of concern about earthquakes. This supports the findings of other studies that it is the personalization of risk that gives rise to concern. In St. Louis, there was a significant relationship in both the 1992 and 1993 surveys between believing that many people in the respondent's neighborhood would be killed in a severe earthquake and earthquake concern. In Cape Girardeau, there was a significant relationship in 1992 between believing that most buildings in one's neighborhood would fall and earthquake concern. This relationship was also present, though not quite statistically significant, in the St. Louis area in 1992. While we cannot conclude that the latter relationship was genuine, the consistency of the correlations between perceived measures of earthquake consequences and earthquake concern suggests that the two are related.

Another relationship that emerged also suggests a linkage between consequences or personal risk and concern. In Cape Girardeau, there was a fairly strong correlation between the item stating that "earthquakes are going to cause widespread loss of life and property whether we prepare for them or not" and concern. Although this was intended as a measurement of fatalism, it obviously also captures a notion of earthquake consequences. In fact, zero order correlations revealed that in the Cape Girardeau sample this item was virtually uncorrelated ($r = -.058$) with the other fatalism/efficacy item, which stated that earthquake preparations will work. These findings together suggest that the consequentiality dimension of this variable was probably more salient than the fatalism dimension: People who see great potential for death and destruction in earthquakes will be more concerned about them.

It should be noted in passing that one of our measures relating to neighborhood consequences, the one stating that one's neighbors would have no idea what to do during an earthquake, was in one instance (Cape Girardeau in 1992) negatively correlated with earthquake concern. This is somewhat contrary to our expectation, but the relationship may reflect a sense that it is the neighbors, not the respondent, that is at risk. Thus, there is little personalization of the risk. In addition, since people tend to generalize their own attitudes, characteristics, and behaviors to others around them (see, for example, Byrne and Blaylock, 1963; Ross, 1977; Ross, Greene, and House, 1977), it may also be that people who feel that they are ready for an earthquake (who also reported a high level of concern) will be less likely to see their neighbors as having no idea what to do. In fact, the zero-order correlations revealed that the sign of the coefficient between believing that one's preparations will work and that neighbors would have no idea what to do is negative, as this argument would suggest. Thus, we do not take the negative relationship of the latter variable to concern as undermining our overall finding that the perceived consequences of an earthquake are a factor influencing earthquake concern.

## Other Factors Influencing Earthquake Concern

Beyond the three key factors outlined above—quake likelihood, efficacy, and perceived quake consequences—there are no consistent relationships across the three geographic areas and two surveys. Two correlations suggest that people of higher socioeconomic status may be less concerned about earthquake risk net of other factors: a negative correlation between education and concern in the St. Louis area in 1992 and between income and concern in Cape Girardeau in 1992. In fact, people of higher socioeconomic status may have less to lose in a major earthquake, even though the opposite would appear to be true, as the value of their property is greater. It is, of course, also true that they are more likely to have earthquake insurance and to live in newer, more earthquake resistant homes. In many of the older, poorer neighborhoods in the St. Louis area, buildings are largely of unreinforced masonry. However, there is no evidence of a relationship between socioeconomic status and concern in any of the other four samples.

Race came close to statistical significance in three of the six samples, but the direction of the relationship was inconsistent. No predictor other than the ones we have discussed had a statistically significant effect in more than one of the six samples. It is notable that earthquake experience, trust in scientists and religious leaders, presence of children, marital status, and gender had no consistent effects. In general, it was the perceived likelihood of a quake, feeling that preparations would work, and perceptions of the personal consequences of a damaging earthquake that gave rise to feelings of concern, with a possible small negative effect related to socioeconomic status.

## Summary and Conclusions

In this chapter, we have examined the conditions and social characteristics that give rise to earthquake awareness, as measured by perceptions about the likelihood of a damaging earthquake in the next ten to fifteen years, and concern about earthquakes. Outside the Browning context, our models did better at explaining concern than they did at explaining awareness. It seems clear not only that the Browning episode increased earthquake awareness in mid-America, but also that those who gave the most credibility to Browning's prediction were the ones who became most aware of the longer-term earthquake risk in the region. Above and beyond the credibility they gave to Browning, those who talked with their friends and neighbors about Browning's prediction reported a higher level of awareness about longer-term earthquake risk than those who did not. In 1992 and 1993, outside the Browning context, our models did not do well at predicting earthquake awareness. However, comparison of our 1992 and 1993 analyses with that of 1990 suggests two potential factors that may increase earthquake awareness: generalized fears about risks ranging from war to natural hazards and unskeptical acceptance of what others, particularly "leaders" and "experts," say. Items that tapped these concepts directly predicted acceptance of Browning's statement and indirectly predicted perceptions about longer-term earthquake risk in the 1990 survey. Both of these factors offer promise for future research on earthquake awareness.

With respect to earthquake concern, three clusters of variables emerge as significant predictors of concern. First, people who feel efficacious rather than fatalistic report higher levels of concern. This suggests that concern is associated with empowerment to do something about a risk, not paralyzing fear. Second, people who think that an earthquake is likely report higher levels of concern. Third, personalization of risk is clearly associated with concern. Those who foresee a strong likelihood of fatalities and the collapse of buildings in their own neighborhoods are more concerned, as are those who see earthquakes as inevitably causing a loss of life. There is a slight tendency among people of higher socioeconomic status to be less concerned about earthquake risk, perhaps because they live in safer environments and are more likely to have insurance.

In an earlier chapter, we explored the relationships among awareness, concern, and preparedness. In the next and final chapter, we shall place those factors in a larger model that examines all of the factors we could identify that directly or indirectly influence how well prepared people are for the damaging earthquake that is coming, sooner or later, to the New Madrid Seismic Zone.

# 7

# Putting It All Together: What Explains Preparedness and How Can It Be Encouraged?

AS WE HAVE SEEN IN EARLIER CHAPTERS, earthquake awareness is an important factor contributing to earthquake concern, and concern, in turn, contributes to preparedness. However, concern is only one factor that influences preparedness. In this chapter, we shall report multivariate analyses of the factors that influence earthquake preparedness, and develop a model illustrating various factors that have both direct and indirect effects on earthquake preparedness in mid-America. We shall also discuss the implications of our findings regarding what can be done to encourage and sustain the preparedness gains that resulted from the Browning prediction.

Earthquake preparedness was defined as the number of possible actions out of a total of fourteen that respondents said they had taken to prepare for an earthquake. These actions are listed in table 4-6 in chapter 4, along with the percentage of respondents who said that they had taken each action in the 1992 and 1993 surveys.

## Predicting Earthquake Preparedness: Eight Hypotheses

Table 7-1 shows the seventeen predictor variables that were included in our initial multivariate analyses of earthquake preparedness. These predictor variables were intended to tap seven dimensions of attitudes, perceptions, and experience, and they are reflected in the organization of table 7-1. Based on our own research on response to the Browning prediction and on research by others on earthquake preparedness, we expected to find greatest levels of preparedness among persons with eight characteristics:

1. People who report being more concerned about the risk of damaging earthquakes and other disasters. In earlier chapters, we examined the relationship between concern and preparedness. As noted then, past research shows a linkage between concern and preparedness, although there are mixed findings on whether that relationship is positive or curvilinear. We found a

Table 7-1. Predictor Variables Included in Multivariate Analysis of Earthquake Preparedness (July 1992 and May 1993)

Concern Issues
    Concern about risk of earthquakes
    Concern about other disasters

Experiential Issues
    Earthquake experience

Perceived Earthquake Likelihood
    Likelihood of earthquake within ten to fifteen years
    Threat of earthquake is overrated

Perceived Earthquake Consequences
    Quake would kill many in neighborhood
    Most buildings in neighborhood would collapse

Perceptions about Neighbors' Preparedness
    Neighbors would have no idea what to do in earthquake
    Neighbors are prepared for earthquake

Efficacy/Fatalism Issues
    Waste to prepare for earthquake
    Preparations for earthquake will work
    Earthquakes will cause loss no matter what*

Sociodemographic Issues
    Race
    Education
    Income
    Marital status
    Own or rent home

*Although this was designed as an efficacy/fatalism item, our later analyses indicated that it was responded to largely as a perception about the consequences of earthquakes.

positive zero-order relationship and believe that concern is a mechanism by which earthquake awareness is transformed into earthquake preparedness. Hence, we expected to find a positive relationship between concern and preparedness even after control for other relevant predictors of preparedness.

2. People who have previously experienced damaging earthquakes. Past research has frequently shown disaster experience to be a significant predictor of disaster preparedness (Mileti, Fitzpatrick, and Farhar, 1992; Turner, Nigg, and Paz, 1986; but see Baker, 1979, for contrary findings). People who have experienced a disaster may have seen firsthand the benefits of preparedness. Hence, we expected that people who had experienced damaging earthquakes would be better prepared than people who had not.

3. People who think a damaging earthquake is likely and that the threat of earthquakes in the region has not been overrated. We have noted in several earlier chapters that much of the effect of the perceived likelihood of an earthquake may be indirect: It influences concern, which in turn influences preparedness actions. It is dubious to what extent it is a direct predictor of preparedness actions. We saw, for example, that believing Browning's earthquake prediction was only weakly related to plans to change schedules in response to the Browning prediction. Here, we include perceived earthquake likelihood to see whether it has any direct effect on earthquake preparedness, or whether its effects are entirely indirect.

4. People who perceive greater consequences of a damaging earthquake in their own neighborhoods. Past research indicates that it is personalization of risk and perceived consequences of a disaster such as an earthquake or hurricane in one's own neighborhood or at one's own home that influence preparedness behavior (Mileti, Fitzpatrick, and Farhar, 1992; Baker, 1979; but see also Turner, Nigg, and Paz, 1986: 187). Accordingly, we expected that people who perceived that a severe earthquake would cause fatalities to occur and buildings to collapse in their own immediate neighborhoods would be more likely than others to prepare for a damaging earthquake. In chapter 6, we saw that these factors were significant predictors of concern; here we seek to see whether they also have an independent, direct effect on preparedness.

5. People who perceive that others around them are taking actions to prepare for a damaging earthquake. We saw in our analysis of response to the Browning prediction that what people perceived their friends and neighbors to be doing was one of the best predictors of what they planned to do in response to the prediction. Similarly, other studies (Mileti, Fitzpatrick, and

Farhar, 1992; Baker, 1979) also have found that perceptions that friends and neighbors are taking protective actions are a good predictor of whether individuals themselves take protective actions against earthquakes or other natural hazards.

6. People who are at the efficacy end of the efficacy/fatalism continuum. In a multivariate analysis of a preparedness index similar to ours, Turner, Nigg, and Paz (1986: 184) found fatalism to be the best predictor of the number of actions taken. It is reasonable to believe that people who feel that what they do will make a difference are more likely to take actions than those who feel that it will make no difference. In fact, research has shown this to be applicable not only to disaster preparedness but also to a wide range of other actions. It may be linked to the concept of internal versus external locus of control: Internal locus of control—believing that one largely controls one's fate—generally leads people to effort and action, while external locus of control has the opposite effect. This has been shown for a variety of actions including other studies of response to the threat of disaster (Sims and Baumann, 1972; Lazarus and Monat, 1979).

7. People of higher socioeconomic status and majority racial background. We included these variables in the analysis because we believe that the resources one has are an important potential influence over the actions one takes. To those who face a daily struggle to make ends meet, preparing for disaster is likely to be a low priority—and one that people lack the resources to address, even if they want to. In their study of earthquake preparedness in Los Angeles, Turner, Nigg, and Paz (1986) found that income and education were positively correlated with preparedness and that white Anglos were more prepared than Hispanics or African Americans.

8. People who are married and own their own home. These variables were included as measures of community investment and of consequentiality of a disaster. Married people have not only themselves to look after but also a spouse, and possibly other family members. Home owners risk losses to their own residential properties that renters do not. And both marriage and home ownership may give people a greater sense of attachment or personal investment in their neighborhood and community—and hence a greater incentive to take protective actions.

The analyses were performed separately for the St. Louis metropolitan area, Cape Girardeau, and Sikeston in each of the two surveys, July 1992 and May 1993. Initially, all variables shown in table 7-1 were included in multiple regression analyses of preparedness in both years. As with our analyses of awareness and concern reported in chapter 6, we then performed more limited analyses including only predictors that attained or approached statistical significance in the preliminary analysis. The results of these analyses are shown in table 7-2.

## Findings

Table 7-2 reveals a number of consistent relationships, and in all six analyses, a substantial portion of the variance in preparedness is explained. The adjusted $R^2$ ranges around .25 in Sikeston, between .25 and .30 in the St. Louis area, and in the .35–.38 range in Cape Girardeau. The best predictors of earthquake preparedness are believing that one's friends and neighbors are well prepared, owning a dwelling as opposed to renting, and being concerned about the risk of earthquakes. The two former variables are statistically significant predictors of preparedness in five of the six analyses, and the latter in four out of the six analyses. All of these relationships are in the expected direction.

In the rare instances in which these variables did not have the expected effects, related variables often did. For example, there was one instance (Sikeston in 1993) in which perceived preparedness of friends and neighbors was not significantly related to earthquake preparedness. In that analysis, however, there was a strong negative effect on preparedness of the other measure of perceptions about neighbors' preparedness: believing that one's neighbors would have no idea what to do in an earthquake. The 1993 Sikeston analysis was also one of just two models in which earthquake concern was not related to preparedness. However, our other concern measure, concern about other natural disasters, was a strong predictor of earthquake preparedness in that model. Based on the strong and consistent effects of concern, perceptions about neighbors' preparedness, and home ownership, we conclude that each of these has a substantial causal effect on earthquake preparedness.

Two other relationships also appear with a fair degree of consistency in the model: socioeconomic status and the efficacy/fatalism dimension. In five of the six analyses, income, education, race, or a combination of those factors have statistically significant effects on preparedness in the expected direction. However, which of those indicators is most related to preparedness varies: Education is significant in three of the six models; income is significant in two

Table 7-2. Regression Analysis of Earthquake Preparedness (July 1992 and May 1993)

| | St. Louis Area | | | | Cape Girardeau | | | | Sikeston | | | |
|---|---|---|---|---|---|---|---|---|---|---|---|---|
| | July 1992 | | May 1993 | | July 1992 | | May 1993 | | July 1992 | | May 1993 | |
| | B | Beta | B | Beta | B | Beta | B | Beta | B | Beta | B | Beta |
| Own or rent home | -.907 | -.171[e] | -1.536 | -.253[f] | -2.003 | -.416[f] | | | -1.174 | -.199[c] | -1.047 | -.179[b] |
| Neighbors are prepared | .851 | .276[f] | .474 | .138[b] | 1.207 | .381[f] | 1.004 | .301[f] | 1.207 | .312[f] | | |
| Quake experience | .936 | .169[e] | .501 | .064 | .551 | .108 | .958 | .158[a] | .406 | .065 | | |
| Quake concern | .956 | .311[f] | .768 | .225[f] | .587 | .278[a] | .896 | .235[c] | .248 | .070 | | |
| Buildings would collapse | .233 | .069 | | | .614 | .179[a] | .398 | .095 | | | | |
| Race | -.699 | -.099[a] | | | -.661 | -.085 | | | | | | |
| Education | | | | | .384 | .150[a] | | | .696 | .239[e] | .628 | .228[d] |
| Income | .265 | .113[a] | .109 | .043 | | | 1.171 | .403[f] | | | | |
| Waste of time to prepare | | | -.962 | -.212[f] | | | | | | | -1.176 | -.302[f] |
| Preparations will work | | | .413 | .091 | | | .592 | .128 | .688 | .146[a] | | |
| Quake would kill in neighborhood | | | -.224 | -.058 | | | | | | | | |
| Quakes cause loss no matter what | | | .209 | .053 | | | | | | | | |
| Concern about other disasters | | | | | | | | | | | .725 | .222[c] |
| Neighbors have no idea what to do | | | | | | | | | | | -1.037 | -.245[e] |
| $R^2$ | .295 | | .283 | | .379 | | .412 | | .260 | | .294 | |
| Adjusted $R^2$ | .281 | | .264 | | .346 | | .383 | | .233 | | .272 | |
| F | 20.833 | | 14.374 | | 11.592 | | 14.225 | | 9.669 | | 13.430 | |
| Significance | .0001 | | .0001 | | .0001 | | .0001 | | .0001 | | .0001 | |
| N | 356 | | 337 | | 141 | | 129 | | 172 | | 167 | |

*Positive coefficient indicates that people of color more prepared.

[a]Significant at .05 level.
[b]Significant at .01 level.
[c]Significant at .005 level.
[d]Significant at .001 level.
[e]Significant at .0005 level.
[f]Significant at .0001 level.

and approaches significance in a third; race is significant in one and approaches significance in another. In only one instance are two of these predictors significant in the same model. The variation from model to model in terms of which socioeconomic status indicator is significant might be attributable to multicolinearity if the three socioeconomic indicators were very highly correlated, but they are not. The strongest intercorrelation coefficient among these variables is .544; in all other cases it is .450 or less. That is not sufficiently strong to cause a colinearity problem. Hence, we conclude that the differences in which the predictor is significant are real but difficult to explain. What is clear from the analysis is that people with higher social status and greater resources tend to be better prepared.

We also found support for the idea that a sense of efficacy raises preparedness, while fatalism inhibits it. In three of the six models, one of our first two measures of the efficacy/fatalism dimension was a significant predictor of preparedness. In St. Louis and Sikeston in 1993, believing that it is a waste of time to prepare for earthquakes had a strong negative effect on preparedness. In Sikeston in 1992, believing that preparedness actions are almost certain to work had a significant positive effect on preparedness, and its positive effects approached significance in St. Louis and Cape Girardeau in 1993. The only fatalism indicator that did not have the expected effects was the belief that earthquakes will cause losses no matter what people do. It had only one effect that approached significance, and that was in the direction opposite what was expected. As discussed in the previous chapter, however, this indicator in retrospect appears to have operated only partly as a fatalism measure: It also appears, as shown in table 7-1, to have operated as a measure of perceived earthquake consequences. That it had no effect is not surprising in light of this interpretation, since fatalism and perceived earthquake consequences were hypothesized to have opposite effects.

Before leaving the issue of the fatalism/efficacy dimension, it is worthy of mention that as an alternative way of measuring this dimension, we constructed a Likert-type scale composed of the three original measures as shown in table 7-1. The three measures were summed with the least fatalistic response being a 1 and the most fatalistic being a 4. Thus, it could range in value from 3 to 12. We then ran the same regression analyses with this variable substituted for the three measures. Its effects were significant in three of the six regressions, but in all but one, adjusted $R^2$ was less than when the variables were included separately.

With respect to other variables, we found some modest effects of earthquake experience in the predicted direction. This predictor had statistically significant effects in two of the six regressions and smaller, nonsignificant effects in three others. Although its signs were consistently in the right direction, it is in most cases a rather weak predictor of preparedness. We did not find much direct effect on preparedness caused by the perceived consequences of an earthquake in the respondent's neighborhood and none at all by the perceived likelihood of a quake. These two variables have indirect effects on preparedness (more so for quake consequences than for quake likelihood) through their contributions to earthquake concern. However, they have little or no direct effect when concern and other relevant variables are held constant.

To summarize, then, we found substantial and consistent positive effects on preparedness from home ownership, the perceived preparedness of neighbors, and concern about earthquakes or other natural disasters. We also found that higher socioeconomic status is associated with better preparedness, though the measure of socioeconomic status thus correlated varies across the times and places we studied. We found some support for the effects of efficacy versus fatalism on preparedness, and a mild tendency for people with earthquake experience to be better prepared. On the other hand, neither perceived earthquake likelihood nor perceived earthquake consequences in the neighborhood appear to have direct effects. Whatever effect these two latter variables have occurs through the intermediary variable of earthquake concern. Thus, of the eight expected relationships listed at the beginning of this chapter, we found support for six. Only items 3 and 4, expecting direct effects of quake likelihood and quake consequences, respectively, are unsupported.

## A Model of Earthquake Preparedness in Mid-America

By combining the results of multivariate analyses reported in this chapter and in chapter 6, we can propose a causal path-type model showing the process through which earthquake preparedness is shaped in the New Madrid Seismic Zone. This model is shown in figure 7-1. The model is based on the overall pattern of findings from the 1992 and 1993 surveys in the three geographic areas studied. The lines and arrows show direct effects, with the thickness of the line approximately proportional to the strength of the effects. In addition to these direct effects, a variable may also have indirect effects through its influence on one or more intervening variables, which in turn have direct effects on other variables. For example, perceived quake likelihood has no direct effect on earthquake preparedness, but it does have an indirect effect through its effect on earthquake concern, which in turn has a direct effect on earthquake preparedness.

As the analysis reported above indicates, there are six predictors that have direct effects on earthquake preparedness. The three with the strongest direct effects are earthquake concern, owning as opposed to renting, and perceptions that one's friends and neighbors are well prepared for an earthquake. Efficacy as opposed to fatalism and high socioeconomic status also have direct effects on preparedness, as, to a minor extent, does earthquake experience. Efficacy

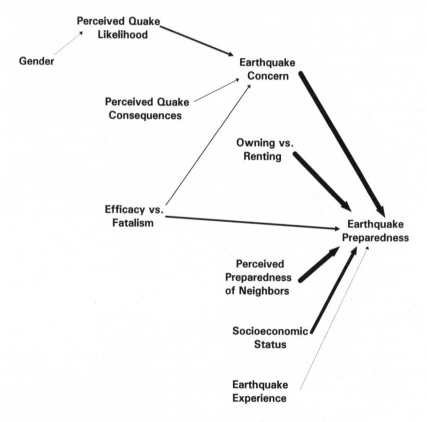

Fig. 7-1. A Model of Earthquake Preparedness in Mid-America

also has an indirect effect on earthquake preparedness, by contributing to earthquake concern. Thus, this predictor has both direct and indirect effects on earthquake preparedness.

It is notable that people's beliefs in the likelihood of a damaging earthquake within the next ten to fifteen years and the consequences they perceive such a quake as having in their own neighborhoods have no direct effect on earthquake preparedness. However, that does not mean that these variables are irrelevant to earthquake preparedness. Both of them do have some indirect effects, because they both contribute to concern, which in turn contributes to earthquake preparedness. We also sought to explain what factors influence people's perceptions about the likelihood of an earthquake. However, the predictors we used explained little of the variance in that factor, except in the context of the Browning prediction, in which believing the Browning prediction did influence people's perceptions about the long-term likelihood of a damaging earthquake in the New Madrid region. Gender did have a consistent but weak effect on the perceived likelihood of an earthquake, and it is included in the model for that reason.

In our modeling, a number of variables were treated as primary factors—that is, we took them as a given and did not try to explain them. This was the case for all sociodemographic characteristics, as well as the efficacy/fatalism continuum, earthquake experience, the perceived preparedness of neighbors, and perceptions about the consequences an earthquake would have in one's own neighborhood. It is evident that if we did try to explain these factors, we would identify additional paths that could be added to figure 7-1. For example, it is reasonable to assume that owning versus renting is influenced by socioeconomic status. Thus, we do not claim that figure 7-1 shows every linkage among this set of variables that might exist; rather, it shows those that we tested for and found evidence to support.

## Maintaining and Enhancing Earthquake Preparedness in Mid-America

What are the implications of our study for efforts to maintain and improve earthquake preparedness in the New Madrid Seismic Zone? We see several. First, a note of encouragement: The effects of the Browning episode were lasting, not fleeting. It had effects on the awareness of earthquake risk, concern about earthquakes, and household preparedness for earthquakes that lasted at least through mid-1993, two and a half years after Browning's prediction had been disconfirmed.

While our study has focused on household preparedness, other research shows that there have been lasting effects on institutional preparedness as well (Olshansky, 1994). Building codes have been improved, earthquake vulnerability studies have been undertaken, and in some cases, major retrofit projects have been begun as well. For example, in May 1995, the state of Illinois completed a $34 million project to make the approaches to an interstate highway bridge over the Mississippi River at East St. Louis resistant to earthquakes (Eardley, 1995). Similar work was planned to begin on the Missouri approaches to the bridge in 1997. Systematic bridge assessment and retrofit programs have been undertaken in Illinois, Kentucky, and Mississippi (Olshansky, 1994).

*What Remains to Be Done?*

While the New Madrid Seismic Zone is better prepared now for an earthquake than it was in the past, it is equally clear that much remains to be done. For example, about 80 percent of buildings in the city of St. Louis are of unreinforced masonry, and many of them are on unstable soil (Bolin, 1993; Allen, 1990). The Federal Emergency Management Agency (1990) has estimated that 20–40 percent of schools and churches in the city would be destroyed in a major earthquake. Other areas, such as Memphis and the portion of the Illinois section of the St. Louis area located on unstable flood plain soils, are also highly vulnerable.

At the household preparedness level, our data show that relatively few people have taken the more difficult and expensive actions to prepare for an earthquake, such as fastening objects, having an engineer's assessment done of their homes, or making structural changes to reduce earthquake hazard. And some have not taken even the easiest steps, such as storing food and water or having battery-powered radios, flashlights, and spare batteries. What can be done to get more people to take these actions?

Some of the answer is suggested by our 1992 and 1993 analyses of earthquake preparedness, and some is suggested by our findings about what happened during the Iben Browning earthquake scare. Our 1992 and 1993 analyses explained a sizable portion of the variance in preparedness. Some of the factors that directly affect earthquake preparedness are subject to influence by policymakers; others are not. Little can be done to change people's level of earthquake experience or the mix of socioeconomic status. Home ownership rates are higher in the Midwest than in other parts of the country, but since a variety of public policies (such as tax law) already support home ownership, it is unclear to what extent that can be changed by public policy. Other factors, however, including earthquake concern, sense of efficacy versus fatalism, and perceptions about the preparedness of friends and neighbors, probably are subject to influence.

*Influencing Preparedness Through Public Information*

The latter factors outlined above—earthquake concern, efficacy, and perceptions about the preparedness of others—are potentially subject to influence by public information campaigns. That is clearly shown by two recent studies of such campaigns in California, as well as by the positive effect on earthquake preparedness of the extensive media attention to the Browning prediction. The first such campaign in California centered around the Parkfield Earthquake Prediction Experiment. Research by Mileti and colleagues (Mileti, Fitzpatrick, and Farhar, 1992, 1990; Mileti and Fitzpatrick, 1993, 1991) shows clearly that this is the case. In fact, these studies showed that characteristics of the message—particularly the number of times and number of different ways in which the prediction was communicated—had larger effects on risk perception and on information-seeking than did personal characteristics. And these message characteristics had a large indirect effect on preparedness through their effects on information-seeking: When people heard about the prediction repeatedly and from a variety of mass media sources, they tended to seek out information on their own, such as by discussing the prediction with their friends. And when they sought information on their own, they were much more likely to take actions to prepare for an earthquake. Mileti, Fitzpatrick, and Farhar (1992) argue that the mailing of a brochure with specific information on what to do to prepare for an earthquake, as well as on the earthquake risk and the reasons for preparing, was especially effective in stimulating information-seeking and heightened preparedness.

Mileti et al. (1993) obtained similar findings when a newspaper insert was distributed in the San Francisco area in September 1990, after seismologists raised the estimated thirty-year probability of a magnitude 7.0 or greater earthquake in the area from 50 percent to 67 percent. Their survey of Bay area residents found that the newspaper insert—when supplemented with similar information from other sources—led people to seek more information about earthquakes, which in turn led them to take actions to prepare for an earthquake.

These findings are consistent with our own findings about the effect of the Loma Prieta earthquake and the Browning prediction in the New Madrid Seismic Zone. Anyone who was exposed to the mass media in the mid Mississippi Valley in 1989 and 1990 received extensive information, which was repeated frequently, about earthquake risks. It came from a variety of sources: newspapers, television, employers, schools, and sometimes local governments. Our 1990 and 1991 surveys indicated that this exposure to information did all of the things that the Parkfield Earthquake Prediction Experiment and the revised Bay area quake probability announcements and their accompanying information campaigns did: It heightened earthquake awareness, gave rise to concern, led people to discuss the risk with their friends and neighbors and to take note of what others were doing to prepare, and led people to take actions to prepare for an earthquake. Knowing that public information campaigns can work, we turn now to a brief examination of what has happened to public information about earthquake risk in mid-America since the disconfirmation of the Browning prediction.

*Trends in Earthquake News Coverage: A Pattern of Surge and Decline*

As noted above, there was a great deal of public information about earthquakes and earthquake risk disseminated in 1989 and 1990. Mass media attention to earthquake risk, some tied to the Browning prediction and some not, clearly contributed to the increase in preparedness that occurred in 1989 and 1990. People were warned about the earthquake risk and told what they could do. For example, the *St. Louis Post-Dispatch* ran a series on preparation for earthquakes in September 1989 and again in October, after the Loma Prieta earthquake. During the Browning scare, it ran a special section on Sunday, October 28, 1990, on how to prepare for an earthquake.

After the flurry of earthquake-related news items in 1989 and 1990, media attention to the earthquake issue declined sharply. To investigate the extent to which that was the case, the indexes of newspapers in the three largest cities in the New Madrid Seismic Zone were examined for all years from 1989 through

1995 for which they were available. These included the *St. Louis Post-Dispatch* (1989 through the first eleven months of 1995), the *Memphis Commercial Appeal* (1990–1995), and the *Southeast Missourian* of Cape Girardeau (1989 and 1992–1995). The number of stories listed in the indexes that in some way pertained to earthquakes or earthquake risk in the New Madrid Seismic Zone were counted. (On the other hand, stories pertaining to earthquakes and earthquake risk in areas other than the New Madrid region were not counted.)

There was slight unavoidable variation in the methods of counting the stories, because the means by which the indexes were arranged varied slightly. For the *Post-Dispatch*, the bound index available in St. Louis–area libraries was searched under the heading "earthquake"; only stories appearing under that subject pertaining to the NMSZ were counted. The Cape Girardeau Public Library's index to the *Southeast Missourian*, which was a bound index for 1989 and a computer database for 1992 and later years, was also searched for items listed under "earthquake." No index was available for 1990 or 1991. In the index to the *Southeast Missourian*, only items pertaining to the Cape Girardeau area were included; thus all earthquake stories in that index (except one about someone from Cape Girardeau assisting in an earthquake elsewhere, which was not counted) pertained to the NMSZ. In both of these indexes, it appears that the articles were indexed only by title; the index includes the title and in some cases a brief summary of the article's contents.

The *Commercial Appeal* has a computerized index that works differently than those of the other two newspapers. In this index, searches are conducted by keywords that appear in the text of the articles rather than by title. The entire text of the article is available on-line at the Memphis Public Library. The index was searched using the keywords "earthquake" and "Memphis." That is, articles containing both of those words somewhere in the article were counted. In all cases in which the title of the story was ambiguous, the article itself was reviewed on-line to determine whether issues related to earthquakes or earthquake risk in the NMSZ were a major topic. Where they were, the article was counted. It is possible that this method may have included articles that would have been missed using the indexes of either of the other two newspapers, since articles were found that focused on the NMSZ earthquake issue but did not reflect that focus in their titles. The *Commercial Appeal* index goes back only to mid-1990.

Figure 7-2 shows the number of New Madrid earthquake-related news items in each of the years from the *Post-Dispatch*; figure 7-3 shows the same information for the *Commercial Appeal*. The data for the *Southeast Missourian* are not presented graphically because of the small number of articles and because of the 1990–91 gap in the data. For the *Post-Dispatch*, there were far more stories in 1989 (forty-seven) and 1990 (ninety-six) than appeared in any year thereafter. Even before the Loma Prieta earthquake, on October 17, 1989, there had been twelve New Madrid earthquake-related items, a number that equals or exceeds the number in any year from 1991 on. Clearly, the Loma Prieta earthquake did lead to more attention, as thirty-five stories ap-

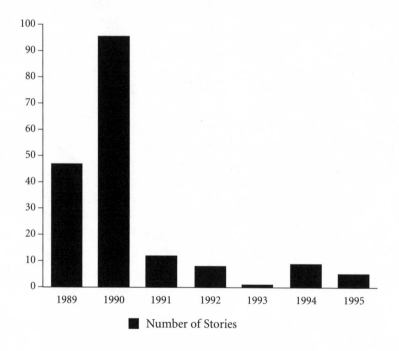

Fig. 7-2. Number of Quake News Stories, *Post-Dispatch*, 1989–1995

peared in the roughly two and a half months that remained in the year after that earthquake.

Not surprisingly, the number of stories is by far the greatest in 1990, the year in which the Browning prediction dominated the news. Just ten of the ninety-six stories that year appeared before the first story about Browning. What is significant is the dramatic falloff after 1990. While the public was bombarded with news items about earthquakes and earthquake risk in the NMSZ in 1989 and 1990, such stories almost disappeared thereafter. There was only one such story listed in the 1993 *St. Louis Post-Dispatch* index. It may be that during that year attention to earthquake risk was forgotten in the face of the record-

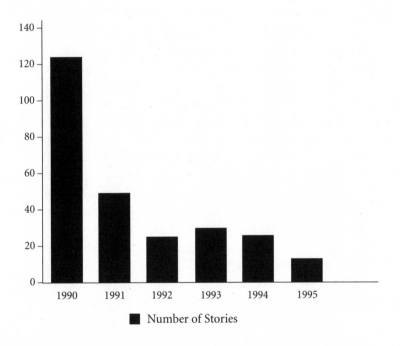

Fig. 7-3. Number of Quake News Stories, *Commerical Appeal,* 1990–1995

setting flood that devastated large regions in the mid and upper Mississippi Valley. The number of New Madrid earthquake stories did increase to nine in 1994. However, three of those were linked to the destructive Northridge earthquake that struck the Los Angeles area on Martin Luther King Day in January 1994; the articles discussed what an earthquake of similar strength might do in the New Madrid region. Moreover, the number of stories decreased again in 1995. Despite the year-to-year variation after 1990, there was no year after 1990 in which the number of New Madrid–related earthquake items in the Index exceeded a dozen.

Although the *Commercial Appeal* did appear to have somewhat more coverage of NMSZ earthquake issues after 1990 than the *Post-Dispatch*, it displayed a similar overall pattern. Because its index does not begin until mid-1990, we cannot assess the effect of the Loma Prieta earthquake on its coverage. However, like the *Post-Dispatch*, the *Commercial Appeal* had far more earthquake-related stories in 1990 than in any later year. Between June 27 (when the database begins) and the end of 1990, the *Commercial Appeal* had 124 stories on earthquakes or earthquake risk in the New Madrid region. In the entire year of 1991, there were forty-nine stories, and many of those appeared early in the year and related to the impact of Iben Browning's failed earthquake prediction. In no year after 1991 were there more than thirty stories, and by 1995 the number of stories had dwindled to just thirteen. There were twenty-four stories in 1992 and twenty-six in 1994; in 1993 there were slightly more, at thirty, but five pertained to the National Earthquake Conference that was held in Memphis in May 1993. Excluding the latter stories, the number of stories each year from 1992 through 1994 amounted to only about two per month. Many of these were brief reports of occasional minor earthquakes in the New Madrid fault zone, typically with magnitudes of around 3.0. They appear to receive more attention in the Memphis newspaper than in St. Louis, probably because the epicenters are usually closer to Memphis. Most of the rest of the stories concerned efforts to retrofit existing buildings or bridges, or the construction of new earthquake-resistant buildings. Such stories undoubtedly have some impact in keeping people aware of the earthquake risk in the region. Nonetheless, even the Memphis newspaper has had relatively few stories on NMSZ earthquake hazard since 1991, and 1995 represented a low point in coverage.

Undoubtedly because it is a much smaller newspaper than either of the others, the *Southeast Missourian* has had the fewest stories on earthquakes in recent years. We could not directly assess its coverage of the Browning event, because the newspaper was not indexed in 1990. However, Spence et al. (1993) do include reprints of an extensive series of articles on earthquake risk and earthquake preparedness from October 1990. What is clear is that the *Southeast Missourian* had very little coverage of earthquake risk or earthquakes in the New Madrid region in 1992 and thereafter. In fact, the number of stories in 1989—twelve—exceeds the total number of stories in the entire four-year period from 1992 through 1995. In no year from 1992 on did the number of stories in the *Southeast Missourian* index exceed five, and in 1993 there were none at all. This pattern suggests two conclusions: First, in Cape Girardeau as in St. Louis, the Loma Prieta earthquake in 1989 did appear to have stimulated heightened attention to earthquake risk in the New Madrid region. Second, the Cape Girardeau newspaper, like its counterparts in St. Louis and Memphis, devoted little attention to the New Madrid earthquake hazard from 1992 on. In fact, it appears to have totally disregarded the issue in 1993.

This analysis suggests that public information on earthquake risk in the NMSZ has been very scarce indeed since 1990. That represents a lost opportunity, and although earthquake awareness and preparedness gains from the Browning event were largely sustained through mid-1993, it raises questions about whether they will be sustained over the longer term. As discussed above, it is clear from research on the Parkfield Earthquake Prediction Experiment and on the public information campaign concerning heightened earthquake risk in the San Francisco Bay area that information campaigns do contribute to increased preparedness. But neither the mass media nor public safety agencies have devoted much effort to conducting public information campaigns about preparing for earthquake risk in mid-America. In light of major flood disasters in the St. Louis area in 1993 and to a lesser extent again in 1995, it is understandable that the attention of public safety agencies was turned elsewhere. But given that lack of attention, combined with what we know about the effects of information campaigns on preparedness, one thing is clear: It is time again for public information campaigns to spur preparedness in the region. We know from experience, both in the NMSZ and in California, that information can spark preparedness. It is time to act upon that knowledge.

## The Implications of Our Research for a New Public Information Campaign

What might such a campaign emphasize? How should it be carried out? We think that our research findings, along with those of others, offer some fairly clear answers to those questions. Certain things are clear from past research, particularly the work of Mileti and colleagues on the Parkfield prediction and the revised Bay area earthquake probabilities discussed above. These studies show clearly that multiple sources are better than single sources, that a direct-mailed brochure or a special newspaper insert is an effective strategy, and that any information campaign must contain specific information about the nature of the risk and what to do about it. Including percentage probabilities of a damaging earthquake is less important than making clear statements to the effect that scientists believe that the risk is great enough that preparation is necessary in order to save lives, prevent injuries, and minimize damage.

Our findings suggest certain things above and beyond this. Our findings clearly established that earthquake concern, sense of efficacy versus fatalism, and perceptions about the level of preparedness of friends and neighbors have direct effects on earthquake preparedness. This suggests a type of message that does two things. First, the message must show people why they should be concerned, and what they can do. Examples might include the following:

If your water heater falls over during an earthquake, it could start a fire that might destroy your home and endanger your family. But you can prevent this by taking the simple step of strapping the heater so it won't fall. Here's how, and here's what you'll need. . . .

If you have a brick chimney, it could collapse during an earthquake. In past earthquakes, collapsed chimneys have been a common cause of damage and injuries inside people's homes. But by going into your attic and nailing down plywood around the chimney, you can greatly reduce the chances of bricks falling through the ceiling and injuring people or damaging possessions in your home. Here's what you need to do. . . .

Did you know that after a major earthquake, you could have no running water for up to three days? Power outages, blocked roads, and temporary shortages could prevent you from being able to buy even basic foods. You can prepare by having a three-day supply of canned food and bottled water. Here's what you'll need. . . .

Major disasters, such as strong earthquakes, tornadoes, and severe ice storms, are going to happen sooner or later in our area. When they do, you could be left without electrical power for a period of up to several days. If that happens, will you have a way to light your house, receive emergency radio information broadcasts, or prepare food for your family? Here's what you'll need to get through the extended power failure that a natural disaster could cause. . . .

The above are examples of information items designed to raise concern by showing people what the consequences of a damaging earthquake could be and, at the same time, telling what they can do to mitigate the consequences. Thus, they are designed simultaneously to increase concern (which has direct effects on earthquake preparedness) and efficacy, which influences earthquake preparedness both directly and indirectly via enhanced concern. These and similar items might be pretested in a focus group or through a survey methodology to see what specific types of wording and information are most effective in enhancing concern and sense of efficacy. Once pretested, they could be included in mailed brochures or newspaper inserts to be distributed in the NMSZ.

Our research also showed that perceptions about the preparedness of other people is a significant predictor of preparedness levels. It also showed that a sizable proportion of the population have taken steps to prepare for a damaging earthquake. For example, we saw in chapter 4 that the average respondent to our 1992 and 1993 surveys had taken between seven and eight of fourteen steps to prepare for a damaging earthquake. Communicating this information to the public could enhance preparedness. Brochures and mass media advertisements showing things that people are doing to get ready for an earthquake could lead to improvements in preparedness, if they convinced people that many others are doing the same. For example, knowing that most of their neighbors have stored food, learned how to turn off their utilities, and stockpiled spare batteries for radios and flashlights could lead more people to take such actions. Emphasis on what others are doing to get ready for an earthquake has generally been absent from public information campaigns to enhance earthquake preparedness. Our research findings suggest that such an emphasis could enhance preparedness.

Similarly, news reports on what people have done to prepare for a damaging earthquake—as well as institutional actions to prepare—could help to enhance preparedness. An example of this can be seen in a front-page *St. Louis Post-Dispatch* story in 1995 about the completion by the state of Illinois of a $34 million project to make a major Mississippi River bridge more earthquake resistant. Our research showed consistently that what people perceive that significant others and social institutions are doing to get ready is an important predictor of preparedness actions. In different ways, we found evidence of this in all four of our surveys. Yet prominently placed earthquake preparedness stories such as the one about the bridge have been relatively infrequent since December 1990.

### The Urgency of a New Public Information Campaign

I have decided to conclude this book with an observation and an exhortation. Many social scientists, journalists, seismologists, and public safety officials were highly critical of mass media coverage of the Iben Browning earthquake prediction. As we have seen, much of that criticism was well founded. However, it is ironic that for all its shortcomings, the coverage did stimulate people in mid-America to learn about and prepare for the damaging earthquake that will sooner or later occur. In contrast to their criticism of the Browning coverage, these media critics have been eerily silent about what may be a greater problem with media coverage: its inattention to the issue of earthquake risk since the disconfirmation of the Browning prediction. Why is this a greater problem? The answer is simple: Continued inattention to earthquake risk inhibits further improvements in preparedness and jeopardizes improvements that have already been attained. While it is true that earthquake preparedness held up quite well into mid-1993 in spite of this inattention, it is not clear that it can hold up forever.

Clearly, in the past the provision of information has played an important role in contributing to earthquake preparedness in mid-America, in Los Angeles, in the San Francisco Bay area, around Parkfield, California, and in other places subject to earthquake risk. In the absence of such information, there is little or no reason to expect that people will take further steps to prepare. And such information has been mostly absent in mid-America since the end of 1990, as is clearly shown in our analysis of newspaper coverage of New Madrid earthquake risk from 1989 through 1995. Some encouraging developments did occur in January and early February of 1996, in the form of two brief flurries of coverage of earthquake issues in the St. Louis and southwest Illinois papers.

The first flurry of coverage was prompted by the 1996 Illinois Earthquake Preparedness Week, held in mid-January. Articles, including some information on what to do to prepare for an earthquake, appeared in the *St. Louis Post-Dispatch*, the *Edwardsville* (Illinois) *Intelligencer*, and the *Alton* (Illinois) *Telegraph*. It appears that the Illinois Emergency Management Agency was quite effective in getting the message out to the press about Earthquake Preparedness Week in 1996. The second flurry of coverage occurred around the beginning of February, when Missouri geologists discovered a new fault, believed to be capable of producing damaging earthquakes, near Cape Girardeau and about forty miles closer to St. Louis than the main New Madrid fault zone. This discovery resulted in another round of newspaper articles and in a news feature series by one television station, the St. Louis ABC affiliate Channel 30, on earthquake risk in the St. Louis area.

These events are highly encouraging, because they represent the most extensive coverage of New Madrid earthquake risk in the St. Louis area since the end of the Browning episode. However, more sustained and extensive attention is still needed. For example, no newspapers have recently published "earthquake safety guides" like the ones distributed during the Browning scare. Moreover, coverage of the earthquake risk has remained sporadic in 1996 and 1997. As this book went to press, I checked the *Post Dispatch*'s Internet site to determine whether there had been any increase in coverage of New Madrid earthquake risk. There has not. Again in 1997, there was a brief flurry of stories about Earthquake Preparedness Week in January. However, even though the newspaper's new Internet archive search detects words in the article as well as words in the title, thereby finding more articles, I could find only fifteen articles on New Madrid earthquakes and earthquake risk in 1996 and just eleven in the first seven months of 1997.

The time for renewed attention to the New Madrid earthquake hazard is now, before the gains of 1989 and 1990 are lost. Past research has told us a lot about how to carry out such an information campaign, and the present study tells us more. To a large extent, we know what to do. But acting on these recommendations requires a cooperative effort of public safety agencies, the disaster research community, and the mass media. An effective effort can ensure that the gains of the past are sustained. The time to begin work on that renewed effort is now.

**References**
**Index**

# References

Ad Hoc Working Group on the December 2–3, 1990, Prediction. 1990. *Evaluation of the December 2–3, 1990, New Madrid Seismic Zone Prediction.* Report to National Earthquake Prediction Evaluation Council (NEPEC), released October 18.

"Aftershock Followed Earthquake." 1968. *St. Louis Post-Dispatch*, November 11.

Allen, William. 1990. "Built on Sand: Soil Type One of Three Major Factors in Damage Done to Buildings." *St. Louis Post-Dispatch*, October 28, p. 10H.

Allen, William, and Thom Gross. 1990. "Quakemania: Some Tremble in Fear, Others Plan to Party." *St. Louis Post-Dispatch*, November 18, p. 1D.

Allport, Gordon W., and Leo Postman. 1947. *The Psychology of Rumor.* New York: Holt.

Atwood, Douglas, Lawrence V. Clark, and Louis Veneziano. 1991. "The Effect of Various Media on Responses to the New Madrid Earthquake Prediction as Moderated by Sociodemographic and Personality Characteristics." Paper presented at the Research Conference on Public and Media Response to Earthquake Forecasts, Southern Illinois University at Edwardsville, May 16–18.

Atwood, L. Erwin. 1993. "Perceived Impact of an Earthquake Prediction: The Third Person Effect." *International Journal of Mass Emergencies and Disasters* 11: 365–78.

Baker, Earl J. 1979. "Predicting Response to Hurricane Warnings: A Reanalysis of Data from Four Studies." *Mass Emergencies* 4: 9–24.

Baldwin, Tamara. 1991. "Earthquake Awareness in Southeast Missouri: A Study in Pluralistic Ignorance." Paper presented at the Research Conference on Public and Media Response to Earthquake Forecasts, Southern Illinois University at Edwardsville, May 16–18.

———. 1993. "Earthquake Awareness in Southeast Missouri: A Study in Pluralistic Ignorance." *International Journal of Mass Emergencies and Disasters* 11: 351–63.

Ball-Rokeach, Sandra. 1973. "From Pervasive Ambiguity to Definition of the Situation." *Sociometry* 36: 378–89.

Beer, Francis A. 1981. *Peace Against War: The Ecology of International Violence.* San Francisco: W. H. Freeman.

Bliss, Mark. 1990. "Schools Get Prepared." *Southeast Missourian*, October 17.

Bolin, Robert. 1993. "Post-Earthquake Shelter and Housing Research Findings and Policy Implications." Chap. 4, pp. 107–31, in *Socioeconomic Impacts*, Committee on Socioeconomic Impacts, Monograph 5, 1993 National Earthquake Conference. Memphis, Tenn.: Central United States Earthquake Consortium.

# References

Bowles, Samuel, and Herbert Gintis. 1976. *Schooling in Capitalist America.* New York: Basic Books.

Byrne, D., and B. Blaylock. 1963. "Similarity and Assumed Similarity of Attitudes Between Husbands and Wives." *Journal of Abnormal and Social Psychology* 67: 636–40.

Byrne, Richard, Jr. 1990. "Earth Quacks." *Riverfront Times* (St. Louis), December 5.

Cantril, Hadley. 1965. *Invasion from Mars.* New York: Harper and Row. [Originally published in 1940.]

Chartered Casualty and Property Underwriters. 1992. *The Earthquake That Didn't Happen.* N.p.: Central Illinois Chapter.

Clark, Lawrence V., Douglas Atwood, and Louis Veneziano. 1993. "Situational and Dispositional Determinants of Cognitive and Affective Reactions to the New Madrid Earthquake Prediction." *International Journal of Mass Emergencies and Disasters* 11: 323–35.

Committee on Awareness, Preparedness, and Public Education. 1993. *Awareness, Preparedness, and Public Education.* Monograph 3, 1993 National Earthquake Conference. Memphis, Tenn.: Central United States Earthquake Consortium.

Couch, Carl J. 1970. "Dimensions of Association in Collective Behavior Episodes." *Sociometry* 33 (1970): 457–71.

Coverman, S., and J. Sheley. 1986. "Change in Men's Housework and Child Care Time, 1965–1975." *Journal of Marriage and Family* 48: 413–22.

Dearing, James W., and Jeff Kamierczak. 1993. "Making Iconoclasts Credible: The Iben Browning Earthquake Predictions." *International Journal of Mass Emergencies and Disasters* 11: 391–403.

de Mann, Anton, and Paul Simpson-Housley. 1987. "Factors in Perception of Tornado Hazard: An Exploratory Study." *Social Behavior and Personality* 15: 13–19.

Dynes, Russell R. 1993. "Social Science Research: Relevance for Policy and Practice." In *Improving Earthquake Mitigation: Report to Congress,* National Earthquake Hazard Reduction Program Reauthorization Act. Washington, D.C.: Federal Emergency Management Agency.

Eardley, Linda. 1995. "Work on Bridge Completed." *St. Louis Post-Dispatch,* June 1, pp. 1, 15.

Echevarria, J. A., K. A. Norton, and R. D. Norton. 1986. "The Socioeconomic Consequences of Earthquake Prediction." *Earthquake Prediction Research* 4: 175–93.

Edwards, Margie L. 1991. "Public Response to the Browning Forecast: Implications for Household Preparedness in Memphis." Paper presented at the Research Conference on Public and Media Response to Earthquake Forecasts, Southern Illinois University at Edwardsville, May 16–18.

———. 1993. "Social Location and Self-Protective Behavior: Implications for Earthquake Preparedness." *International Journal of Mass Emergencies and Disasters* 11: 293–303.

Farley, John E. 1988. *Majority-Minority Relations.* 2d ed. Englewood Cliffs, N.J.: Prentice Hall.

———. 1990. *Sociology.* Englewood Cliffs, N.J.: Prentice Hall.

———. 1993. "Public, Media, and Institutional Responses to the Iben Browning Earthquake Prediction—Editor's Introduction." *International Journal of Mass Emergencies and Disasters* 11: 271–77.

———. 1994a. "Twentieth Century Wars: Some Short-Term Effects on Intergroup Relations in the United States." *Sociological Inquiry* 64: 214–37.

———. 1994b. "Sustained Preparedness or Cry Wolf? New Madrid Earthquake Awareness and Preparedness Trends, October, 1990–May, 1993." In *Earthquake Awareness and Mitigation Across the Nation: Proceedings*, vol. 3, 1055–65. Fifth U.S. National Conference on Earthquake Engineering, Chicago, July 10–14. Oakland, Calif.: Earthquake Engineering Research Institute.

Farley, John E., Hugh D. Barlow, Lewis G. Bender, Marvin S. Finkelstein, and Larry Riley. 1991a. "Earthquake Hysteria: Public Response to a Pseudoscientific Forecast of Disaster." Paper presented at the annual meeting of the Midwest Sociological Society, Des Moines, April 11.

Farley, John E., Hugh D. Barlow, Marvin S. Finkelstein, and Larry Riley. 1993. "Earthquake Hysteria, Before and After: A Survey and Follow-up on Public Response to the Browning Forecast." *International Journal of Mass Emergencies and Disasters* 11: 305–21.

Farley, John E., Hugh D. Barlow, Marvin S. Finkelstein, Larry Riley, and Lewis G. Bender. 1991b. "Earthquake Hysteria, Before and After: A Survey and Follow-up on Public Response to the Browning Forecast." Paper presented at the Research Conference on Public and Media Response to Earthquake Forecasts, Southern Illinois University at Edwardsville, May 16–18.

———. 1991c. "1990 Midwest Earthquake Scare: Public Response to a Pseudoscientific Forecast of Disaster." Paper presented at the UCLA International Conference on the Impact of Natural Disasters, Los Angeles, July 9–12.

Federal Emergency Management Agency. 1990. "Estimates of Future Earthquake Losses for St. Louis City and County, Missouri." *Earthquake Hazards Reduction Series* 53, Central United States Earthquake Preparedness Project, Memphis, Tenn.

Franklin, Stephen. 1990. "Quake Preparation Becomes Big Business in Midwest." *Chicago Tribune*, November 18, sect. 1, pp. 1, 14.

Gordon, Jennifer. 1990. "Town Mostly Quiet on Quake Day." *Arkansas Gazette*, December 4.

Gori, Paula L. 1993. "The Social Dynamics of a False Earthquake Prediction and the Response by the Public Sector." *Bulletin of the Seismological Society of America* 83: 963–80.

Hamilton, R. M., and Arch C. Johnston. 1990. *Tecumseh's Prophecy: Preparing for the Next New Madrid Earthquake*. N.p.: U.S. Geological Survey Circular 1066.

Hirose, Hirotada. 1986. "The Psychological Impact of the Tokai Earthquake Prediction: Individual's Responses and the Mass Media Coverage." *Japanese Psychological Research* 28, no. 2: 64–76.

Hirose, Hirotada, and T. Ishizuka. 1983. "Causal Analysis of Earthquake Concern and Preparing Behavior in the North Izu Peninsula." *Japanese Psychological Research* 25: 101–11.

# References

Hochschild, Arlie. 1989. *The Second Shift: Working Parents and the Revolution at Home*. New York: Viking Penguin.

Hopper, Margaret C., ed. 1985. "Estimation of Earthquake Effects Associated with Large Earthquakes in the New Madrid Seismic Zone." U.S. Geological Survey Open File Report 85-457. Denver, Colo.: U.S. Geological Survey.

Hyman, Herbert H., and Charles R. Wright. 1979. *Education's Lasting Influence on Values*. Chicago: University of Chicago Press.

Hyman, Herbert H., Charles R. Wright, and John Shelton Reed. 1975. *The Enduring Effects of Education*. Chicago: University of Chicago Press.

Johnston, Arch C., and Susan J. Nava. 1985. "Recurrence Rates and Probability Estimates for the New Madrid Seismic Zone." *Journal of Geophysics Research* 9: 6737–53.

Katz, Elihu. 1957. "The Two-Step Flow of Communication: An Up-to-Date Report on an Hypothesis." *Public Opinion Quarterly* 21: 61–78.

Kennedy, John M. 1991. "Hoosier Reactions to the Predictions of an Earthquake." Paper presented at the Research Conference on Public and Media Response to Earthquake Forecasts, Southern Illinois University at Edwardsville, May 16–18.

Kerckhoff, Alan C., Kurt W. Back, and Norman Miller. 1965. "Sociometric Patterns in Hysterical Contagion." *Sociometry* 28: 2–15.

Kerr, Richard A. 1991. "The Lessons of Dr. Browning." *Science* 253: 622–23.

Kohn, Melvin L. 1969. *Class and Conformity*. Homewood, Ill.: Dorsey.

Kunreuther, Howard. 1993. "Earthquake Insurance as a Hazard Reduction Strategy: The Case of the Homeowner." Chap. 7, pp. 191–210, in *Socioeconomic Impacts*, Committee on Socioeconomic Impacts, Monograph 5, 1993 National Earthquake Conference. Memphis, Tenn.: Central United States Earthquake Consortium.

Landa, Marinell. 1990. "Missouri National Guard, State Workers Stage Earthquake Drill." *St. Louis Post-Dispatch*, December 2, p. 11A.

La Piere, R. T. 1934. "Attitudes Versus Actions." *Social Forces* 13: 230–37.

Lazarsfeld, Paul F., Bernard Berelson, and Hazel Gaudet. 1944. *The People's Choice*. New York: Duell, Sloan, and Pearce.

Lazarus, R. S. 1996. *Psychological Stress and the Coping Process*. New York: McGraw-Hill.

Lazarus, R. S., and A. Monat. 1979. *Personality*. 3d ed. Englewood Cliffs, N.J.: Prentice Hall.

Levenbach, F. David, and David E. England. 1991. "Citizen Preparedness for the December, 1990 Earthquake." Paper presented at the annual meeting of the Southwest Political Science Association, San Antonio, Tex., March 27–30.

Li, Jinfang. 1991. "Social Responses to the Tangshan Earthquake." Paper presented at the UCLA International Research Conference on the Impact of Natural Disasters, Los Angeles, July 9–12.

Lofland, John. 1985. *Protest: Studies of Collective Behavior and Social Movements*. New Brunswick, N.J.: Transaction Books.

Major, Ann M. 1991. "The 'Situational' Nature of Situational Communication Theory: Opinion Responses Before and After the Browning Earthquake Prediction of 1990."

Paper presented at the Research Conference on Public and Media Response to Earthquake Forecasts, Southern Illinois University at Edwardsville, May 16–18.

———. 1993. "A Test of Situational Communication Theory: Public Response to the 1990 Browning Earthquake Prediction." *International Journal of Mass Emergencies and Disasters* 11: 337–49.

Mazon, Mauricio. 1984. *The Zoot-Suit Riots: The Psychology of Symbolic Annihilation.* Austin: University of Texas Press.

Mikami, Shunji, and Ken'ichi Ikeda. 1985. "Human Response to Disasters." *International Journal of Mass Emergencies and Disasters* 1: 107–32.

Mileti, Dennis S., JoAnne D. Darlington, Colleen Fitzpatrick, and Paul W. O'Brien. 1993. *Communicating Earthquake Risk: Societal Response to Revised Probabilities in the Bay Area.* Fort Collins: Colorado State University, Hazards Assessment Laboratory and Department of Sociology.

Mileti, Dennis S., and Colleen Fitzpatrick. 1991. "How to Issue and Manage Earthquake Risk Information: Lessons from the Parkfield Earthquake Prediction Experiment." Paper presented at the Research Conference on Public and Media Response to Earthquake Forecasts, Southern Illinois University at Edwardsville, May 16–18.

———. 1993. *The Great Earthquake Experiment: Risk Communication and Public Action.* Boulder, Colo.: Westview Press.

Mileti, Dennis S., Colleen Fitzpatrick, and Barbara C. Farhar. 1990. *Risk Communication and Public Response to the Parkfield Earthquake Prediction Experiment.* Final report to the National Science Foundation. Fort Collins: Colorado State University, Hazards Assessment Laboratory and Department of Sociology.

———. 1992. "Fostering Preparations for Natural Hazards: Lessons from the Parkfield Earthquake Prediction." *Environment* 34, no. 3: 16–39.

Mileti, Dennis S., J. Hutton, and J. Sorensen. 1981. *Earthquake Prediction Response and Options for Public Policy.* Institute of Behavioral Science. Boulder: University of Colorado.

Mileti, Dennis S., and Paul W. O'Brien. 1992. "Warnings about Disaster: Normalizing Communicated Risk." *Social Problems* 39: 40–57.

Miller, David L., Kenneth J. Mietus, and Richard A. Mathers. 1978. "A Critical Examination of the Social Contagion Image of Collective Behavior: The Case of the Enfield Monster." *Sociological Quarterly* 19: 129–40.

Moore, Harry E. 1964. *. . . And the Winds Blew.* Austin: University of Texas, Hogg Foundation for Mental Health.

Mulilis, John-Paul, and T. Shelley Duval. 1991. "The Impact of Nearby Earthquakes on Individual Earthquake Preparedness." Paper presented at the UCLA International Conference on the Impact of Natural Disasters, Los Angeles, July 9–12.

Nigg, Joanne. 1987. "Factors Affecting Earthquake Threat Awareness and Response." Paper presented at the Pacific Conference on Earthquake Engineering, New Zealand, August 5–8.

Nishenko, S. P., and Gilbert A. Bollinger. 1990. "Forecasting Damaging Earthquakes in the Central and Eastern United States." *Science* 249: 1412–16.

# References

Olshansky, Robert B. 1994. "Earthquake Hazard Mitigation in the Central United States: A Progress Report." In *Fifth U.S. National Conference on Earthquake Engineering, Proceedings*, vol. 5, 985–94. Oakland, Calif.: Earthquake Engineering Research Institute.

Olson, Richard Stewart, with Bruno Podesta and Joanne M. Nigg. 1989. *The Politics of Earthquake Prediction.* Princeton, N.J.: Princeton University Press.

Pesce, Carolyn. 1990. "Fault Line's Threat Hits Fever Pitch." *USA Today*, November 28.

Qijia, Zou, Su Tuo, and Ge Zhizhou. 1990. *Social and Economic Survey on the Tangshan Earthquake.* Beijing: China Academic Books and Periodicals Press.

"Quake Damage Minor; Felt over Wide Area in Midwest and East." 1968. *St. Louis Post-Dispatch*, November 10, pp. 1A, 6A.

Rose, Jerry D. 1982. *Outbreaks: The Sociology of Collective Behavior.* New York: Free Press.

Rosengren, Karl E., Peter Arvidson, and Dahn Sturesson. 1975. "The Barseback 'Panic': A Radio Programme as a Negative Summary Event." *Acta Sociologica* 57: 309–14.

Ross, Lee. 1977. "The Intuitive Psychologist and His Shortcomings: Distortions in the Attribution Process." In *Advances in Experimental Social Psychology*, vol. 10, edited by Leonard Berkowitz, 173–220. New York: Academic Press.

Ross, L., D. Greene, and P. House. 1977. "The False Consensus Effect: An Egocentric Bias in Self-Perception and Attribution Processes." *Journal of Experimental Social Psychology* 13: 279–301.

Shibutani, Tamotsu. 1966. *Improvised News.* Indianapolis: Bobbs-Merrill.

Shipman, John M., Gilbert L. Fowler, and Russell E. Shain. 1991. "Iben Browning and the Fault: Newspaper Coverage of an Earthquake Prediction." Paper presented at the Research Conference on Public and Media Response to Earthquake Forecasts, Southern Illinois University at Edwardsville, May 16–18.

Shipman, Marlin, Gil Fowler, and Russ Shain. 1993. "Whose Fault Was It? An Analysis of Newspaper Coverage of Iben Browning's New Madrid Fault Earthquake Prediction." *International Journal of Mass Emergencies and Disasters* 11: 379–89.

Showalter, Pamela S. 1991a. *Field Observations in Memphis During the New Madrid Earthquake "Projection" of 1990: How Pseudoscience Affected a Region.* Natural Hazards Research Center, Institute of Behavioral Science, Working Paper No. 71. Boulder: University of Colorado.

————. 1991b. "Small Community Response to the New Madrid Earthquake Prediction: Preliminary Survey Results." Paper presented at the Research Conference on Public and Media Response to Earthquake Forecasts, Southern Illinois University at Edwardsville, May 16–18.

————. 1993a. "Prognostication of Doom: The Effects of an Earthquake Prediction on Four Small Communities." *International Journal of Mass Emergencies and Disasters* 11: 279–92.

————. 1993b. "Prognostications of Doom: Exploring Response to Predictions of Impending Earthquakes." Ph.D. dissertation, University of Colorado at Boulder.

———. 1994. "A Guide for Responding to Unconventional Earthquake Predictions." In *Fifth U.S. National Conference on Earthquake Engineering, Proceedings*, vol. 5, 1035–44. Oakland, Calif.: Earthquake Engineering Research Institute.

Sims, J. H., and D. D. Baumann. 1972. "The Tornado Threat: Coping Styles of the North and South." *Science* 176: 1386–91.

Spence, William, Robert B. Herrmann, Arch C. Johnston, and Glen Reagor. 1993. *Responses to Iben Browning's Prediction of a 1990 New Madrid, Missouri Earthquake*. U.S. Geological Survey Circular 1083. Washington, D.C.: U.S. Government Printing Office.

Stevens, Jill D. 1993. "An Association of Circumstance: The 1990 Browning Earthquake Prediction and the Center for Earthquake Research and Information." *International Journal of Mass Emergencies and Disasters* 11: 405–20.

Sylvester, Judith. 1991. "Media Research Bureau/Suburban Journals Earthquake Prediction Poll." Paper presented at the Research Conference on Public and Media Response to Earthquake Forecasts, Southern Illinois University at Edwardsville, May 16–18.

Turner, Ralph H. 1993. "Reflections of the Past and Future of Social Research on Earthquake Warnings." *International Journal of Mass Emergencies and Disasters* 11: 453–68.

Turner, Ralph H., and Lewis M. Killian. 1987. *Collective Behavior*. 3d ed. Englewood Cliffs, N.J.: Prentice Hall.

Turner, Ralph H., Joanne M. Nigg, and Denise Heller Paz. 1986. *Waiting for Disaster: Earthquake Watch in California*. Berkeley: University of California Press.

Uhlenrock, Tom. 1990. "Nothing Shaking: Schools, Shopping Centers Have Slow Day." *St. Louis Post-Dispatch*, December 4.

U.S. Bureau of the Census. 1992. *1990 Census of Population*. General Population Characteristics, Missouri. Report No. 1990-CP-1-27. Washington, D.C.: U.S. Government Printing Office.

———. 1993. *1990 Census of Population*. Social and Economic Characteristics, Missouri. Report No. 1990-CP-2-27. Washington, D.C.: U.S. Government Printing Office.

Wenger, Dennis E., and Jack M. Weller. 1973. "Disaster Subcultures: The Cultural Residue of Community Disasters." Preliminary Paper no. 9. Columbus: Ohio State University, Disaster Research Center.

Wetzel, Chrisopher G., Edward Hettinger, Robert McMillan, Monroe Rayburn, and Andy Nix. 1991. "When a Quack Predicts a Quake: College Student Reactions to a Disconfirmed Prediction." Paper presented at the Research Conference on Public and Media Response to Earthquake Forecasts, Southern Illinois University at Edwardsville, May 16–18.

———. 1993. "Methodological Issues in Studying Response to the Browning Prediction of a New Madrid Earthquake: A Researcher's Cautionary Tale." *International Journal of Mass Emergencies and Disasters* 11: 437–52.

Zhang, Cui-xia, and John E. Farley. 1995. "Gender and the Distribution of Household Work: A Comparison of Self-Reports by Female College Faculty in the United States and China." *Journal of Comparative Family Studies* 26, no. 2: 195–205.

# Index

# Index

# Index

# Index

John E. Farley is a professor of sociology at Southern Illinois University at Edwardsville. He is the author of *Majority-Minority Relations* (third edition, 1995), *Sociology* (fourth edition, 1998), and *American Social Problems: An Institutional Analysis* (second edition, 1992) and was the guest editor for an issue of the *International Journal of Mass Emergencies and Disasters* focusing on social responses to the Iben Browning earthquake prediction. He was born in Waterloo, Iowa, received his undergraduate education at Michigan State University, and completed his graduate studies at the University of Michigan.